INDIAN ART IN MIDDLE AMERICA

Pre-Columbian &

Contemporary Arts and

Crafts of Mexico,

Central America and

the Caribbean

Frederick J. Dockstader

INDIAN ART IN MIDDLE AMERICA

PHOTOGRAPHY BY CARMELO GUADAGNO

New York Graphic Society  Publishers, Ltd.

GREENWICH, CONN. U.S.A.

Frontispiece: Plate 18

FIGURE OF A SEATED WOMAN

Library of Congress Catalogue Card Number 64-21815

PRINTED IN ITALY 1964   8789646

*Entire Book Printed by Amilcare Pizzi S.p.A.
Design by Sophie Adler*

To

ROBERT T. HATT
who opened the door
to a whole New World.

In acknowledgment of
his friendly encouragement
and wise guidance,
this book is
affectionately dedicated.

TABLE OF CONTENTS

ACKNOWLEDGMENTS

In the preparation of any reference volume, no one walks alone; those who have gone before smooth and straighten the road, and those who remain contribute through their own studies, while providing encouragement and friendly debate. I am particularly conscious of my indebtedness to both; in the space allotted, only a small proportion of this help can be acknowledged. Since the titles included in the Bibliography form in themselves one indication of assistance received, I add only those persons most intimately connected with this study.

A most pleasant opportunity is provided here to remark on the surprising degree of friendly coöperation which I encountered while organizing the material included in this book. Rarely have I experienced such enthusiastic assistance, much of which went far beyond the usual professional requirements—the proverbial Latin American courtesy indeed communicated itself to everyone connected with the effort! I am, therefore, particularly pleased to acknowledge my warm indebtedness to those persons below who have contributed in varying manner to this publication:

Mr. Herbert Schutz and Mr. Burton Cumming of the New York Graphic Society, whose patience and confidence remained unfaltering;

Mr. Ferdinand Anton, whose excellent photographic skills were matched only by his willingness to share of his field work;

Mr. John S. Williams, who was so instrumental in the initial encouragement and support of the project during its early development;

Mr. Francis E. Ross, whose interest and generosity were repeatedly displayed in providing specimens of particular note, and in taking photographs of material in Panama;

Mr. and Mrs. Neville A. Harte, whose kindness in providing field notes and material filled a particular gap in the Panamanian section;

Mr. and Mrs. Fred Zengel, whose photographic efforts were so enthusiastically and capably undertaken in behalf of this work;

Together with other friends who contributed in so many ways, even though some of these may not have realized at the time how their knowledge was being made use of. Among these should be included Dr. Samuel K. Lothrop, Dr. and Mrs. Matthew W. Stirling, Dr. Irving Rouse, Dr. Edwin M. Shook, Dr. Gordon F. Ekholm, Dr. Stanley H. Boggs, Mrs. Elizabeth K. Easby, Mr. and Mrs. Donald J. Leonard, and Dr. and Mrs. Kurt Stavenhagen.

For the use of photographs and data involving various specimens included in this volume, I am happy to acknowledge the courtesy of these individuals and their institutions:

Dr. Linton Satterthwaite, Curator, and Miss A. Frances Eyman, Assistant Curator, American Section, and the University Museum, Philadelphia, Pennsylvania;

Dr. William R. Coe, Director, and Miss Háttula Moholy-Nagy, Research Assistant, and the Tikal Project, University Museum, Philadelphia, Pennsylvania;

Dr. Robert Wauchope, Director, and the Middle American Research Institute, Tulane University New Orleans, Louisiana;

Dr. J. O. Brew, Director, and Mrs. Katherine Edsall, Registrar, and the Peabody Museum, Harvard University, Cambridge, Massachusetts;

Dr. Robert Goldwater, Director, and the Museum of Primitive Art, New York;

Dr. Gordon F. Ekholm, Curator of Middle American Archeology, and the American Museum of Natural History, New York;

Mrs. Jane Rosenthal, Curator of Primitive Art, and the Brooklyn Museum of Art, New York;

Mr. Ralph T. Coe, Curator, and Mr. G. F. Crabtree, Jr., Assistant Curator, Native Arts Department, and the Nelson Gallery-Atkins Museum, Kansas City, Missouri;

Dr. James L. Swauger, Assistant Director, and Dr. Don W. Dragoo, Curator, and the Carnegie Museum, Pittsburgh, Pennsylvania;

Mr. Francis W. Robinson, Curator, and the Detroit Institute of Arts, Detroit, Michigan;

Mr. Richard D. Collins, Director, IBM Gallery of Arts and Sciences, New York;

Miss Calinda Colón, Research Assistant, and the Universidad de Puerto Rico, Río Piedras, Puerto Rico.

Throughout our travels in Middle America prior to this study we had occasion to visit with and to enjoy the hospitality of many, many persons whose friendship, interest and assistance we treasure; I cannot allow this to go unnoted, although the names of these friends are so many as to be impossible to record here. I can only extend a heartfelt *muchísimas gracias* to each of these, and to publicly acknowledge the professional courtesies of the following:

Dr. Daniel F. Rubín de la Borbolla, Director, and the Museo de Artes Populares, Mexico City, Mexico;

Dr. Eusebio Dávalos Hurtado, Director, and the Instituto Nacional de Antropología e Historia, Mexico City, Mexico;

Mrs. Doris Heyden and Dr. Luís Aveleyra Arroyo de Anda, of the Museo Nacional de Antropología, Mexico City, Mexico;

Mr. A. Hamilton Anderson, Archeological Commissioner, Belize, British Honduras;

Dr. Carlos Samayoa Chinchilla, Director, and the Instituto Nacional Indigenista, Guatemala City, Guatemala;

Dr. Antonio Tejeda F., Director, and the Museo Nacional de Arqueología, Guatemala City, Guatemala;

Dr. Tomás Fidias Jiménez, Director, and the Museo Nacional "David J. Guzmán," San Salvador, El Salvador;

Mr. Carlos Balser, and the Museo Nacional de Costa Rica, San José, Costa Rica;

Dr. Alejandro Méndez P., Director, and the Museo Nacional de Panamá, Panama City, Panama;

and to those many individuals in each institution who helped so importantly in handling materials, supplying information, and performing the myriad tasks connected with such a venture. I regret they must remain anonymous.

To Mr. Charles O. Turbyfill, Curator of the Research Branch, Museum of the American Indian, I can only use this means of expressing my appreciation for the years of care which he has given the collections of that institution.

And to Mr. William F. Stiles, and Mrs. Mary W. Williams, of the Museum of the American Indian, my warm thanks for their continuing friendly help during the preparation of this book.

But most particularly, I wish to acknowledge the day-to-day labors of Mr. Carmelo Guadagno, staff photographer of the Museum of the American Indian. His patience and care in taking and re-taking photographs of specimens in the Museum collection to fit the particular requirements of this book is evident throughout its pages; but these fail to show his willingness to go far beyond the usual duties of a photographic collaborant. For the work of Mrs. Jeanne Armel, my secretary, in carrying out typing duties and aiding in lightening the office load, I extend my thanks. Lastly, but by far most vitally, is my wife, Alice, who shared the burdens of several field trips, carried the usual impedimenta in her string bag throughout Middle America, while she took photographs, jotted down data, climbed pyramids and slid down ruins — all without complaint. I can only thank her for her patience and fortitude, and hope she will feel this book a sufficient reward.

Frederick J. Dockstader *Director*
Museum of the American Indian, Heye Foundation

INDEX OF ILLUSTRATIONS

INDEX OF ILLUSTRATIONS

[11]

[13]

PREFACE

The art world of the American Indian can be divided into three primary regions paralleling the geographical composition of the Western Hemisphere. Within these, certain common factors seem to hold true, even though many scattered variations continue to perplex the art historian. Just as the peoples themselves defy sharp classification, any attempt to catalogue Amerindian material culture is bound to expose broad bands which overlap such arbitrary boundaries. Regardless of this seeming contradiction in terms, it is quite possible to examine the art expression of these several regions as entities, each of which justifies individual attention.

For the purpose of this work, the treatment of the Indian art of Middle America is defined as including the visual aesthetic expressions of the indigenous peoples in the area between the northern boundary of Mexico and the southern boundary of Panama. For geographic convenience, this is extended to include the West Indies, even though anthropologists usually do not consider these islands as within the concept of Middle America.

This volume grew out of the earlier publication, *Indian Art in America,* which was devoted to the arts and crafts of the North American Indians, and logically continues that same organization and general approach. Whereas that book tended to emphasize ethnological material in greater proportion than archaeological, in the present work the reverse is true. Two-thirds of the specimens date to the period before the arrival of Columbus, simply because the proportionate survival of aesthetically significant archaeological material far outranks the ethnological.

It is manifestly not possible to include even a small amount of the art expressions of this region, whose population exceeded that of North America several times over. Not only does the limitation of space prevent such an intensive survey, but time has joined with a hostile climate to remove many of the more perishable aspects of early Middle American Indian art. There remain almost no textiles or featherwork, and we have only a very few examples of art in mosaic, shell, wood, or paint, as against the great quantities which we know once existed. As for music, dancing, drama, or literature—all of these are lost; some survivals in present-day practice may represent ancient customs, but one can only guess at the purity of such remnants. Some durable materials, such as gold, have survived; but man has aided nature in the removal of much of this artistic evidence.

The selection attempts to include all of the major regions of Middle America and the West Indies in some degree of cultural depth. Not all types of these art expressions can possibly be considered—their number is far too great—but it can be said that no important geographical area or major cultural period is omitted. Indeed, one of the primary values of this book is the presentation of several areas which rarely receive the attention they merit in art studies devoted to the New World; I am confident that among these latter will be several surprises for those interested in Indian art.

Since sculpture was one of the great interests of the ancient artists of this region, it must be recognized that this again outweighs most of the other arts in the present collection.

While interesting points of comparison between groups will be suggested, it is not proposed to investigate the many facets of cultural diffusion, nor will emphasis be given such problems as transpacific contact; aside from an occasional mention, this is more properly left to analytical studies of art style. The realm of art theory, at best an educated guess, possesses too little evidence in this region to warrant consideration at the present time. This volume is an attempt to gather together some of the finest examples of Middle American Indian art, plus aesthetically outstanding specimens of everyday craftsmanship, in order to introduce the reader to the life of the Indian of the region.

The illustrations are assembled from a variety of public institutions. Originally it had been my fond hope that the resources of the various national museums of the Middle American republics could be included in some depth. Time, distance, and technical problems of photography combined to make this impracticable, although it was possible to draw upon these collections to a limited extent. Nor was it possible to canvass all major North American institutions, although a sampling of specimens from many has been included.

The greater proportion has been frankly and quite deliberately selected from the collections of the Museum of the American Indian, Heye Foundation. This was dictated not only by convenience, and the knowledge of their high quality, but even more by the fact that they are less well known than they should be. Many oft-published classics will be missed by students; to achieve freshness, they have been omitted in favor of less familiar but equally remarkable masterpieces. The bibliography on pp. 217-220 makes reference to these readily available. I hope that the omission of these old friends will be more than compensated by the pleasure of marking new acquaintances. No privately owned material has been included, in the thought that readers should be able to see for themselves such objects as may intrigue them, and in order to encourage greater exploration of public museum resources in the Americas. Unfortunately, this decision admittedly means that some particularly fine specimens have had to be left out of this book.

An effort has been made to present sufficient ethnographic information to enable the reader to understand the origin and function of each specimen, wherever such usage is known. It is my earnest hope that this volume will not only introduce many readers to a new world of art, but will also provide some pleasant surprises to connoisseurs.

INTRODUCTION

THE INDIAN ARTIST AT WORK

A consideration of American Indian art—or that of any alien tradition, for that matter—requires the viewer to divorce himself from previously established criteria; he must endeavor to get as close to the basic viewpoint of the artist as he reasonably can. Only by making such an effort can he hope to gain any sort of understanding of what the person is trying to accomplish. Although it may be quite true that " art is art," the goals, timing, techniques, and approaches often make great differences between the art of one region and that of another—and, most particularly, affect the ability of the alien viewer to judge these creations fairly.

Thus, while much of the sculpture of ancient Middle America might be readily understood by readers trained in European sculptural traditions, certain other plastic expressions would require considerable study before an appreciation was achieved. Furthermore, work in different media might wholly evade such a viewer. This would not mean that either the viewer or the artist was "wrong"; it would simply indicate the differences in the two art concepts.

For, not only is the Middle American Indian art world far removed in time and distance, but the basic purposes behind much of the art production was at variance with European art ideals. Human goals are much the same the world over, yet we strive for them along different paths. Sometimes these paths closely parallel each other; equally often they are extremely disparate. It is this factor of difference which is most frequently difficult for Westerners to accept; there is an unfortunate attempt to find a common denominator, which is all too often a leveling-down process.

In attempting to establish this common ground with the Indian artist, we cannot pretend to view these works through his eyes, however much we may try—nor can we apply his thinking, since even the basic functions of many of the examples included in this book are unknown. This means, particularly in prehistoric Amerindian art, that we are indeed viewing it from afar. The fact that we examine with interest and often with real excitement is one of the greatest tributes we can pay; rarely are we dispassionate. We must of necessity speak in terms of what is left to us, realizing that this is at best only part of the story. Indeed, many present-day judgments would surely have to be reversed entirely, if the whole picture were suddenly to unfold.

Only in recent years has the interest in Middle American art become keen. Although the early Spanish explorers took examples back to Europe which stirred such critical appraisers as Albrecht Dürer and Benvenuto Cellini, the greater interest was in the intrinsic value, in monetary parlance, of the gold and jewels that were displayed; aesthetics played little part in such appreciation. In the four intervening centuries, the interest that was expressed continued to be in mundane terms. It was not until the middle of the last century that the cultural achievements of the Middle American Indians began to enjoy any real degree of recognition. With the 400th anniversary of the discovery of America, a major presentation of Middle American art, mostly from Mexico, was held in Madrid; the Columbian Exposition in Chicago at that same time also included major displays of ancient indigenous art from south of the border. These two exhibitions did much to solidify the interest that early publications by Kingsborough, Squier, Charnay and others had engendered.

But it was not until the next generation that general public acceptance and enthusiasm were awakened. Beyond the small group of devotees one always finds in the front ranks of the art world, Indian art from this region remained little known, just as the area's archaeology itself was but vaguely familiar. With increased knowledge and scientific excavation, interest was aroused and that interest has kindled a glowing flame that now warms many an art gallery and museum hall: there are few art institutions which do not boast some presentation of "Pre-Columbian art," however modest.

As yet, we do not know when man first came into Middle America; Tepexpan Man, once thought to be the oldest human remains in the region, is being rapidly superseded by new discoveries. As of this moment of writing, there is little doubt that people were active in Mexico at least 10,000 B. C. Datable evidence of comparable antiquity for the more southerly regions and the West Indies has not yet been found; it would seem unlikely that they were as settled, although it is entirely possible that excavations in Guatemala or Panama or Ecuador will present us with some surprises.

From the simple flaked-stone beginnings to the classic periods of these cultures, one can realize an amazingly rich variety of artistry at work. The many plates presented in this collection can only hint in barest detail at the extremely wide range of human ingenuity in design and form. There is almost no artistic concept which is not to be found within the area concerned.

It is popular to speak of "high cultures of America" in this context; what are these supposedly superior civilizations? Usually the reference is to the Aztec, Maya, and/or Inca peoples—occasionally the speaker will be aware of related Mixtec, Zapotec, Nazca, or Mochica cultures—and the implication is that they were a race somehow removed...a group of demigods, as it were. We have little knowledge of other civilizations which came and went; tantalizing remains often hint at great cultural achievements which have almost entirely disappeared. One such mystery is

that of the Olmec civilization—if it be a civilization, rather than an art style—which has left behind some of the most remarkable aesthetic expressions, coupled with extreme antiquity. (Plates 26 and 78).

Concepts and Characteristics. What are the characteristics of Middle American Indian art? What is it by definition—indeed, can it be defined? Such questions are far easier to ask than to answer, yet it is that indefinable something that permits the initiated to recognize a given work as being from that and no other area of the world.

When an "art expert" examines an object from a given area, in an attempt to identify it, he eventually bases that identification upon a combination of clues. The manner in which a material is treated; the material itself; the techniques employed to achieve a given result; the style of decoration; the types of ornamentation added; the colors used, singly or in combination; the over-all form; and lastly, the function of the object itself. All of these serve to enable the individual to draw upon his experience. Perhaps one other factor may come into play: the negative factor of *what is not found*; since it is just as important in judging art to be aware that certain areas do *not* do things in a given way.

As a gross generalization, Indian art in Middle America can be summarized as having a preoccupation with clay figurines, particularly with those "doing things;" a great interest in face masks, wide manufacture and use of various types of incense-burners; clay musical instruments in great numbers, particularly whistles; a love of stone for its own sake, and an unusual ability to coördinate design with the natural form of the stone. We cannot accurately judge color sense, since the colors have to a great extent been lost; but the pottery examples we do have which retain their original paint would indicate a strong sensitivity, as in Plate 140. Humor is prevalent, as is a sense of the macabre. Erotic themes are rare, although they exist in scattered regions.

In design concept, there is less in common; in some regions the Indian artist tended to avoid the so-called 'horror of a vacuum' by filling in blanks wherever possible; in other areas, his work was quite plain and simple (Plates 177 and 118); a love of the grotesque is common in some areas, yet is paralleled by complete sophistication in others (Plates 100 and 63).

But a basic love for form in itself is everywhere evident. In some areas this is plain, powerful and bulky (Plate 22); in others, elaboration becomes so marked that the fundamental form is almost lost (Plate 138).

Perhaps one other generalization may be realized, and this is the tendency toward applied decoration, particularly in the ceramic arts. It is true of other media, of course; but most evident in pottery.

In sum, there is no one criterion: Middle American Indian art is a composite of many factors combining to create a form of visual expression which, in the main, exists nowhere else. And it is this fact that makes it an identifiable concept. While it is true that there are the occasional parallels which cause students of human migration to knit their brows, even in these closely related instances there is a quality which remains "Indian" as against any of the alien characteristics.

Area and Environment. There are several terms by which this general region is known. *Mesoamerica,* coined by Paul Kirchhoff in 1943, was helpful to anthropologists interested in the area, but it excludes southern Central America; this latter term is inappropriate for our purposes, since it, in turn, excludes Mexico. And neither (nor indeed *Middle America*) considers the West Indies. I have therefore fallen back on the usage of Middle America and the West Indies as the more exact description of the region in question.

The Middle American region varies geographically almost as much as any in the world. Usually thought of as being a hot, steamy tropical jungle region, it is that—but it is also arid desert country lacking any green cover; it is a high, volcanic mountain range, crisp and cold—and a forest lowland with heavy undergrowth, humid and enervating. In ancient times, the mild and inviting plateau regions held most of the population, as today; but many of the least likely areas were also widely inhabited, as evidenced by archaeological remains. Some of these may have been more favorable to habitation in earlier times, but in all likelihood they were equally uninviting then, and were occupied only as sanctuary by those too weak to defend better homesites.

Some parts of the West Indies are lush and arable, but many only served as temporary stopping places in ancient times—just as today's plane touches down for a gulp of fuel before soaring on to more hospitable spots. But withal, there were very few regions in all of Middle America where man did not pause, however briefly. And this is equally true today.

There seems little correlation between the environment and the degree of cultural expression. One finds "high" and "low" civilizations in all areas; great sections are still unexplored territory, in which ample opportunity awaits future archaeological work. Just as in early times it was possible for a tribe to isolate itself and remain hidden for generations, there are still pockets of indigenous peoples who have seen almost no White men. Lack of transportation is much of the reason for this isolation, and changes will of course come as roads intrude.

How an artist develops often tells much about his environment, since he will tend to reflect the world in which he lives. Indifference to the arts may not stop an artist—but it will certainly affect his work. If his is a strongly religious environment, his work will normally reflect a spiritual quality; if not, then the secular will be portrayed by a more materialistic expression.

In Middle America, much the same took place. It is difficult not to believe that in making such objects as in Plates 13 and 105, the artist did not enjoy a warm welcome from his fellows. Indeed, the creator of the masterpiece in Plate 193 must have basked in the glow of many awe-struck admirers when they saw this for the first time.

The astonishing variety and quantity of small clay whistles, ocarinas, and related musical instruments would suggest that here was a world of happiness, regardless of the burdens each person had to carry. Yet such instruments could also produce plaintive monotones and funereal dirges; though we can produce the same tones ourselves, with the composers gone we have no idea of what was played on these apparently lively little instruments. It is unlikely that these were all for children; many are quite complex, and playing them well would challenge an adult.

And certain it is, that the great number of artistic creations found in the tombs throughout Middle America would prove, if nothing else, that here was an active world; indeed, one wonders if the clay workers ever slept! The tens of thousands of small figurines alone suggest tremendous numbers of potters at work making nothing else. And it is equally certain that popular demand was there; for in time, these could no longer be produced by hand modeling. To satisfy the market, clay workers turned to the wholesale manufacture of figurines by means of molds.

This world, then, was not a somnolent, casual way of life —nor was it a bleak, barely eked-out existence. It was a busy, thriving, active world, in which everyone in it had his work to do. There were merchants hustling to and from, developing commercial interests; there were artisans manufacturing the goods sold by those merchants, and there were soldiers spreading the political boundaries of their group ever farther. We often forget the existence of the little boys and girls who played with the toys that were made for them, and tooted the many delightful little whistles as they ran about. But over all of these people were the wealthy nobles and priests, for whom most of the aesthetically superior objects were created. Without these latter there would probably be very little reason for a volume of this nature.

Cultural Identity. To attempt to attach tribal identification to these ancient political entities is dangerous. When terms such as Tarascan, Totonac, or Chorotega are used, the immediate implication is one of relationship to contemporary Indian tribes living in the same, or adjacent, areas. This is not always true, nor can we even demonstrate the degree of accuracy involved. For example, we do not really know whether the prehistoric peoples of Nayarit spoke the same tongue as the Cora, who live in that state today—yet the latter tribe calls itself " Nayarit." What did their ancestors call their home area? There were great migrations going on all during the many centuries of Middle American prehistory during which large groups entered, rested, and moved on; they left tantalizing but often largely inconclusive evidences of their life behind them. And as one group moved in on another, political membership changed, if not blood lines; thus the Zapotec of one period become the Mixtec of another, in a sense. Any use of tribal terms is uncertain at best, and is but an attempt to indicate a quasi relationship between ancient and modern folk inhabiting a common geographical location.

Therefore not only the period, but even the differing cultural patterns affect our ability to catalogue. There is not any very rigid "tradition" in Middle American art; at best we have only certain patterns of style by which we attempt to classify cultural expressions—but even these are subject to tremendous diversity. And to make the matter more complex, new cultures continue to show up; as excavations are pursued in previously untested areas, more and more hitherto unknown art styles are uncovered. Even in some of the older well-known sites, such as Teotihuacán, as archaeological work expands in depth and extent, new and unusual forms are revealed. To be sure, this all increases our knowledge—but it also often only adds to our confusion.

Linguistic classification is a major field of research in anthropology, but it has limited application in archaeology, for who can analyze ancient Olmec speech patterns? Unless demonstrable links are present, contemporary language forms usually mean little in studying prehistory. The map on page 50 defines the major tribal groups of contemporary Middle America. Not only does it indicate the variety of tongues to be found there, but the extremely complex pattern is only further evidence of the great antiquity and wide-ranging movements of these peoples. Many of these languages are dying out today, and as population and settlement pressures increase, this expiration rate will hasten. The Lacandón remnants in southern Chiapas present a dramatic example of this problem.

It is unwise to attempt to assay the "purest" group in any cultural region. One can say with little fear of contradiction that there are no absolutely pure-blood aborigines in Middle America today; any effort to establish such purity can usually be contradicted by graphic evidence of interrelationship someplace or sometime, however minimal. While there are isolated population segments who have managed to retain a relatively high freedom from intermixture scattered throughout Middle America, their numbers are not large, and all of them have received some proportion of alien blood. Perhaps the major centers of relatively unadulterated blood lines are among the Indians of Panama and Guatemala.

In Mexico, the large Indian population has had a long history of infusion from non-Indian folk, and just as it can be said that there is no Indian in Mexico without some proportion of White blood in his veins, neither is there any white Mexican who lacks Indian blood, aside from very recent European émigrés. In truth, this is a *mestizo* land in which blood mixture can be seen at its best. Although Harrington found a small enclave of quasi-Indian people in a remote part of Cuba, there is actually no Indian culture as such remaining in the Caribbean region. These people were thoroughly decimated after White arrival, and the few remnants carry only a trace of Indian blood, and even less of Indian cultural activity.

What has this to do with Indian art? Simply that the identifications of many of the specimens in this volume are of necessity based upon geographic, rather than cultural, divisions. To attempt to indicate the tribal origin of such specimens would be almost impossible. It is only with objects of recent manufacture, most particularly Plates 209 to 248, to which any satisfactory tribal relationship can be attached. A further stumbling block in using provenience for many of the truly fine archaeological masterpieces in this, or any similar book, is that they have gone through many hands, and in such process, any possibility of tracing their true origin has long been lost. The problem of intrinsic value has made this even more difficult for students.

Indeed, this point could be expanded into a thesis: much of what we *think* we know of Middle America is based upon the alleged provenience of certain key objects; yet this provenience often cannot be proven. Far too little scholarly excavation in proportion to the vast ruins existing in Middle America has been undertaken; without such controlled investigation, source means little. The *huaquero* never reveals his source, and more often he will attach a completely false label in order to mislead the competition —and the scholar.

There is no need to digress into the matter of fraudulent specimens other than to remark that here again, scholarly errors have been made, based upon previously accepted specimens. Nor are they few in number; I doubt that there is a single collection of consequence today which lacks such examples. Many are so masterfully created that they defy detection, and a few are regularly used as examples of the finest aesthetic accomplishments of the ancient craftsman. It is this latter factor of creating an unsound basis for analysis that makes them dangerously misleading. And, since their number is on the increase, so is this danger.

The Functional Aspect. A major point in the consideration of Indian art—or any art, for that matter—is that of function. Concerning the material included in this volume, it can be said that almost every one, if not all, of these objects were made to be used, or to " do something." They were appreciated for their beauty, and this was a recognized function; but it is equally certain that they had a service

to perform. The vessel illustrated in Plate 170 would seem to have no obvious function, at least to us, other than that of simple beauty. It cannot hold anything; it cannot serve to "do anything" other than to look nice. On the other hand, the specimen in Plate 145 can be enjoyed visually, but it also had a definite use.

And these forms and functions change from time to time. It is likely that the regular bowl shape combined with the effigy form, and eventually both became one, as seen in Plate 157. Finally, one sees the ultimate of this in Plate 13 which retains the opening once a major part of the bowl, but otherwise has assumed a completely different characteristic. In function it could no longer serve as a container.

Children were apparently given special place in this art world, for objects were made especially for their use. Miniature vessels, tiny replicas of full-size objects, were provided so that the child could " play house," perhaps even as today. The two wheeled toys in Plate 47 could probably not be regarded as other than for amusement, yet they are attractively designed, and would please any small boy as he walked along the street tugging the little animal behind him.

But the combination of social, religious and economic functions were the primary goals for the prehistoric artists. It would seem that most of these artistic creations were intended for presentation to the gods, or as burial offerings. This is one reason why so many perfect, unused bowls are recovered from graves; the regular practice of making pottery for no other purpose than to be buried with the dead is a blessing to contemporary art history. Offerings to the gods drew out the finest abilities the artisan had to offer.

Wealthy nobles, eager to display their newest acquisition to social rivals—even as collectors today—continually exhorted the artist to even greater production of fine material. Many of these objects were made to be sold; there is no question that art had an economic value in early times, and that artists made a living by the creation of beauty. We know little about the basis of this commerce, but it was similar to the village markets of present-day Mexico, if we can judge by the accounts of Spanish eyewitnesses. Many of the objects sold were used to impress the neighbors; many were used at home for utilitarian or display purposes, and others were carried afield in trade. Art was on a sound economic basis; of this we can be sure, if for no other reason than the combination of high quality and large quantity. Some artists were apparently employed on a full-time basis by wealthy people to assure a regular flow of fine material for their homes and to serve as gifts.

Sources of Design. This, one of the most difficult of all questions to discuss, can never really be settled. We have no way of tracing all of the movements of early man; and it was through these migrations that he gave as well as received many of the inspirations used in his art. It is only by visual comparison that we can analyze prehistoric designs, and such visual deduction can be dangerous. It is a great temptation to regard similarity in design as being proof of alien contact—and it is just as unwise to refuse to examine such possibilities dispassionately—but it will only be by long and exceedingly astute investigation that we will be able, if ever, to arrive at anything like an acceptable theory of design origins.

At the present writing, the question of transpacific contact has dominated discussion in this field. The voyage of the *Kon Tiki* has surrounded the expedition with a romantic aura which has all but obscured the actual accomplishments of that venture. The summary reports and theories which have resulted from this effort have been published by Thor Heyerdahl elsewhere. Suffice it to say that this did demonstrate that ancient transpacific voyages were entirely feasible. There seems no doubt whatsoever that these voyages did take place, and involved several areas of the Pacific; whether these were on any regular basis, rather than occasional, seems less certain. I cannot believe that a measurable, scheduled trade existed between the Americas and the transpacific regions to any great extent prior to 1500, but I am certain both sides of the ocean knew the other existed, and had developed a goodly amount of information concerning each other. As for transatlantic contact, this seems less probable, other than the occasional involuntary visit of a storm-swept vessel.

The commonality of certain widespread concepts found throughout Middle America in religion, social custom, art, architecture, and warfare prove that ancient man was not static. The degree of intertribal trade that went on was far greater than is generally realized. Regular trade routes existed, far more effective than the as-yet-unfinished Pan-American Highway. And, just as merchants or travelers would bring new ideas with them into a given area, so would they take away ideas for use elsewhere. Designs on objects traded introduced those designs into alien regions, and formed a permanent reference file for artists.

Of equal interest, and perhaps just as significant, is what was *not* spread by such travel and trade. One tends to look for common influences, often overlooking the simple obvious object which, once seen, would have been expected to have enjoyed immediate acceptance. Why were these sometimes rejected? Did cartels exist, to prevent just such spreading of prized possessions or trade secrets? Were there religious sanctions, trade rivalries, social controls, or was it simply a lack of raw materials necessary to the manufacture? We will never know—but it is hard not to speculate.

Origins of style in art are never easy to determine. It is easy to make the observation that Casas Grandes pottery design (Plates 2 and 3) is closely related to that of the southwestern United States; yet it is not so easy to determine which was the primary influence. And the various forms of figurines, as shown in Plate 33, must have developed from a central core. Where was that heartland? These are far too sophisticated to have sprung full-blown from the single site in which we find them; there must have been antecedents. What, or where, were they? A glance at the figurine classification established many years ago by Vaillant demonstrated the interrelationship of these. Although many new forms have come to light since, these all fit neatly into that formula. Caso and Bernal have attempted much the same thing in the classification of Zapotec funerary urns (Plate 51); in time, many more such groupings may be developed. It seems that the Jaina style of modeled figurines could be worked into just such an organization, for example.

And, among all of these formulas, the matter of absolute duplication immediately strikes the viewer. One can line up a hundred clay figurines, stone effigies, or masks, or certain types of pottery objects, and the net effect is that of a master hand at work. This point has been made elsewhere in discussing Mimbres pottery; it is no less true of the artistry of the Chupícuaro, Tlatilco, Veracruz, Coclé, Guápiles, or Copán peoples. Were there stables of artists, all of whom followed the style of the master? This is not entirely impossible, for while we can detect technical differences from one hand to another, there was certainly a model which all of the artists in a given group duplicated as faithfully as talent allowed. Moreover, in these exact duplications, careful examination indicates the same hand at work, over and over again. Brush technique, sureness of stroke, design composition, and manipulation are so precisely duplicated as to remove any doubt that the same hand made both objects.

In mold-made work, of course, this is a different matter; but in freehand work, it becomes an interesting point to consider, for if this be true, and I am convinced it is, it would seem true that we may be judging some of these ancient cultures by the work of a single individual (or a very small group) within that culture.

Sex and Religion. The rôles of men and women within these ancient worlds are difficult to establish. Who wove—men or women? What difference did this make in the design and form of the textile? In North America, Hopi men weave; five miles away, Navajo women weave essentially the same general textiles. Did this same situation obtain in ancient Middle America? Was pottery made by men, or women? In contemporary Middle America, both sexes work in clay. What effect did this have upon the output? Were there restrictions on sex; that is, did men make figurines and women make vessels, for example? Such proscriptions do exist in Indian cultures. If only men were allowed to make "ceremonial" designs, and women made "secular" patterns, somewhat as in Plains Indian art, this would explain some of the problems in ancient Indian art practices.

Erotic art is not common in Middle America. Phallic forms, usually in stone, are known, but their use is less familiar. The erotic motif in clay is strongest in western Mexico, particularly in Colima, where modeled figurines with pronounced phallic characteristic are found. Some proportion of erotica is known in central Mexico and Veracruz, and the figurine of the Old Man and the Young Maiden is certainly well known in Mayan pottery. This aspect seems less prevalent the farther south one goes, but it never dies out completely. If eroticism in art is so very common in some Indian areas such as the Peruvian Highlands, the Arctic of the Eskimo, or the Southeastern United States, why does it seemingly skip so lightly over these vast central areas? While one can say that it is not absent anywhere, it is true that it is extremely scarce in many parts of Middle America.

But the strongest of all forces on Middle American art in that of religion. Probably two-thirds of the objects in this volume had a religious function of some sort. This is not surprising, for it seems certain that the religious life of the American Indian tended to be an around-the-clock activity then as now.

It is an oversimplification to read too much into some of these works; are the grotesque forms seen in Plates 100 and 181 expressions of religious devotion, representations of old gods or spirits, or are they simply bizarre designs which the artists enjoyed making just for fun? We can fall into a trap here by attempting the popular pastime so often used in analyzing Indian art: namely, that everything he does in his art is "symbolic." While it is perhaps true that the lack of a formalized alphabetic writing system made his art tend to be more expressive of ideas, thereby rendering it graphically communicative to a great extent, it by no means follows that he reduced everything to symbols when he painted. He was as prone to doodling, scrawling meaningless curlicues, and filling voids with untranslatable designs as any artist today.

In rendering homage to his gods, he did follow certain art patterns, as the plates illustrate. The tremendous degree of duplication in *incensarios,* urns, figurines, and painted representations of deities demonstrates this preoccupation. Many of these were intended as temple offerings, altar vessels, replicas of a particular divinity, or reminders of certain ceremonial activities. Some were accessory objects, to be used in conjunction with rites. As such, extreme pains were taken to produce as aesthetically fine objects as could be made. We can trace the rise and fall of religious force with this very skill in execution; indeed, the power of the priesthood is reflected in the forms, designs, and qualities of the objects manufactured. And as the religious factors wane, there is apparently less concern with fine sacred art, for mold-made objects appear, detail becomes secondary, and eventually many of these erstwhile delicately worked objects begin to appear as slipshod, mass-produced articles with almost no skill apparent in their design or execution.

The "Pre-Columbian" Concept. This brings us back to our own way of looking at much of this work. Previously, the suggestion was made that it is imperative to view this art without European reference, if any depth of understanding is to be achieved. It is equally true that the context of "preciousness" must be removed. These were human beings, who made bad art just as much as they made good art; their work should be regarded as that, and nothing more. The use of the term "Pre-Columbian art" is unfortunate, in the sense it is popularly used today. To most unthinking art devotees, the term refers to the work of the Aztec, Olmec, Mixtec, *et al.*, peoples of Mexico, and the Inca, Chimú, or Nazca folk of Highland Peru. Such references do not, at first blush, usually include the coeval cultures lying between those centers, nor do they include the prehistoric art expressions of North America and the West Indies. Thus the term has taken on a specialized pseudo-art context with little to recommend, and much that is objectionable.

By definition, Pre-Columbian art in America includes all aesthetically significant works made by Amerindian artists prior to 1492. This, no more and no less. This would then be purely a chronological category which would make sense. To restrict it is only to make it an artificial boundary which constricts just as much as it confuses. Further, it tends to remove the works from the Indian category, and makes of the art an expression without human attachment.

In this volume, then, the term, when used, refers solely as an indication of time span. From Plate 1 through 208, every article illustrated is an example of Pre-Columbian art. Those from 209 through 248 are Post-Columbian; this differential is important only in that it places a degree of limit upon European art influences, or the use of certain technical materials and tools.

The use of *Colonial,* often used to cover the period *circa* 1500-1800 (varying with the particular country), is of value primarily in indicating the art forms which were most heavily influenced by Spanish (or Portuguese) tradition. In this volume, Colonial art has been almost totally excluded, in order to more strongly emphasize Indian expression.

Again, *Pre-Columbian* has become popular primarily as a synonym of sorts for *Primitive* in discussing indigenous art. Many persons object to the latter term, and have adopted the former as being less objectionable. But the two are not synonymous, and both give rise to considerable confusion. Each has gray areas of partial or mis-application and when used by nonspecialists, both are quite misleading. Unfortunately, no better phrase has yet been developed which answers all needs. For the purpose of this and related studies, the term *Indian Art* is exactly what is meant, and need be defined further only by specific time period or region.

It seems particularly unfruitful to attempt to establish definitions for such artificial terms as *Primitive Art,* for this is too much a subjective matter; what is one man's primitive is another's sophistication, and time span or regional spread is often confused in such definitions.

Fad and fashion levies a considerable toll in the art of any region—European, American, or Asian. And so it is with this material; if the gods who destine the contemporary art world decide that Mayan art is " in," then equally fine material from the Huástec peoples, or the lowland Cocle-sanos, enjoys less acceptance. This is only to say that it seems unfortunate that much of the basis for the judgment of art is social rather than aesthetic. Perhaps some of the examples in this volume will serve to introduce fads and fashions in less-known regions.

THE PROBLEM OF CHRONOLOGY

The effort to establish dates for Amerindian art objects is a major problem, for it is only with written records that anything like relative accuracy can be achieved, and few of the aboriginal peoples of Middle America developed this skill. A brief word concerning the accomplishments which have been made thus far in archeological dating may help the reader to understand the problems involved, and will also indicate a few of the promising developments just ahead.

When A. E. Douglass discovered that certain trees in the Southwestern United States add growth rings in proportion to rainfall, he created the science of *dendrochronology*, or tree-ring dating. By counting these rings " in reverse," one can find the date when the tree was cut down; the accumulation of many overlapping samples permits the archaeologist to establish many computations, such as the date of a given building, or when a ruin was first built. This was the most successful early step in amassing a body of data relevant to the presence of early man in North America, and enjoyed general acceptance. Unfortunately, this technique does not work universally, since many trees do not increase their growth in such an obliging fashion as do the members of the *Pinaceae* family.

Out of atomic experimentation undertaken during World War II, Willard W. Libby developed *radiocarbon dating*, which relies upon the fact that Carbon 14 is present in all organic matter. Since this deteriorates at an even rate following death, it follows that by measuring the amount of C14 in a bit of shell, bone wood or similar archeological material, a date can often be computed for such an object.

As techniques and the delicate measuring instruments improve, this system is proving to offer increased accuracy, and it has now overcome much of the skepticism which greeted its early appearance. It is still far from producing pinpoint accuracy, but it does give an indication of chronology which seems better than anything previously known—and, more importantly, it can be used throughout the world, thus overcoming a disadvantage of tree-ring computation. Unfortunately, it has two serious drawbacks: it can be thrown off badly by contamination from radioactive sources, and it cannot be applied to non-organic materials. Most of the dating in the archaeological section of this volume has taken advantage of the most recent C14 datings wherever possible.

Other dating techniques have been introduced in recent years with varying degrees of promise. The method known as *thermoluminescence* offers considerable help in dating pottery, if it becomes perfected; this is a complicated process involving the microscopic examination of re-fired pottery. Since potsherds are so widespread, so relatively stable, and have long been such an integral part of archaeological theory, it is obvious that once this system matures, the whole science of archaeology will advance a major step forward. But, at the present writing, this system seems to offer many more problems than promises. The technique of *obsidian hydration* may provide a help in those areas where obsidian was commonly used by man; the major area in which experimentation has been most active is in the Americas, and the results offer cause for considerable optimism. *Pollen analysis* is yet young, but as scholars learn more about this effort to profit by the use of nature's deposits, it may prove to be suitable for those regions which support such examination. One last experimental technique, *glottochronology*, has shown an amazing ability to indicate relative age simply by an indication of how long it takes man to change his speech patterns. This has provided some astonishing insights into prehistory, even in some areas where the language has disappeared; in those regions where a continuum can be established, the results are even more remarkable.

As man refines his devices for measuring time, other techniques surely will develop; but as of today, these seem the most frequently employed attempts to answer the age-old question of how long ago man came into the Western Hemisphere. And it is well to point out that these dates change almost daily; those printed herein are an effort to establish the "latest word" on chronology, realizing that even as this book is printed, many will have undergone revision. That this is no simple matter is illustrated by comparison of any of the dozens of books in print today which deal with Middle America: although nearly all of them present elaborately worked-out chronological tables, almost no two will agree.

Man's attempts to record his history are rare in Middle America; unfortunately, writing was developed in only two major areas, and we have yet to discover a "Rosetta stone." Of the writings of the early peoples, only the Maya, the Mixtec, and the Aztec folk left any considerable bodies of visual communication; these were the targets for destruction on a scale so intense that there are only three examples of Mayan writing extant today, and perhaps two score Mixtec-Aztec books still survive of the thousands burned when the notorious Bishop De Landa destroyed the libraries. Stone glyph-carvings exist in great numbers, but they are as yet not completely decipherable, and tantalize more than they enlighten.

The calendrical systems of Middle America attained a height unrivaled in ancient history, enabling us to place events in a relative, if not absolute scale. On a few Aztec specimens it is possible to pinpoint dates (Plate 23); with those Mayan specimens bearing glyphic dates, the chronology depends upon which of the two major correlations are followed by the reader: that developed by Herbert J. Spinden, or the one established by J. T. Goodman, Juan Martínez Hernández, and J. Eric S. Thompson. The two differ by some 650 years, that of Spinden being the earlier. No other system of correlation has appeared to rival these; contemporary opinion is increasing in favor of the Goodman-Martínez-Thompson chronology, which is followed in the present volume.

With the arrival of the Spaniards, events can be dated by reference to readily translated historical documents. Our primary source is the great *Historia general de las cosas de Nueva España,* by Fray Bernardino de Sahagún. Written between 1565 and 1569 from oral accounts obtained from natives, Sahagún delved into every facet of Mexican life. He tells us how the artisans worked, their techniques and customs, and gives us a picture of the social, economic and political life of the times. Even though earlier accounts, such as the contemporary *Historia Verdadera de la Conquista de la Nueva España,* by Bernal Díaz del Castillo, give much information concerning the period of earliest European contact, none are as encyclopedic.

The balance of what little is known today comes from translations of *códices, lienzos,* Spanish *relaciones,* and such dictionaries and linguistic studies as remain. Just how little we actually possess is revealed whenever we try to interpret the role of a given object in ancient Middle American society; often we can only hazard a vague guess.

The Chronological Table below covers only those regions and cultures included in this volume: based upon the general consensus of the contemporary archeological dating, it is an effort to suggest the time relationship of these cultures to each other.

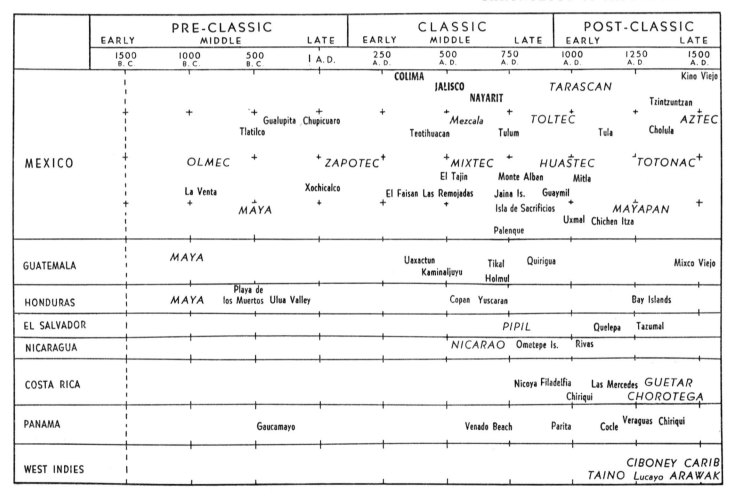

	PRE-CLASSIC			CLASSIC			POST-CLASSIC		
	EARLY	MIDDLE	LATE	EARLY	MIDDLE	LATE	EARLY		LATE
	1500 B.C.	1000 B.C.	500 B.C.	1 A.D.	250 A.D.	500 A.D.	750 A.D.	1000 A.D.	1250 A.D.	1500 A.D.

MEXICO — COLIMA, JALISCO, NAYARIT, TARASCAN, Kino Viejo, Tzintzuntzan, Gualupita, Chupicuaro, Mezcala, TOLTEC, AZTEC, Tlatilco, Teotihuacan, Tulum, Tula, Cholula, OLMEC, ZAPOTEC, MIXTEC, HUASTEC, TOTONAC, El Tajin, Monte Alban, Mitla, La Venta, Xochicalco, El Faisan, Las Remojadas, Jaina Is., Guaymil, MAYA, Isla de Sacrificios, MAYAPAN, Uxmal, Chichen Itza, Palenque

GUATEMALA — MAYA, Uaxactun, Kaminaljuyu, Tikal, Holmul, Quirigua, Mixco Viejo

HONDURAS — MAYA, Playa de los Muertos, Ulua Valley, Copan, Yuscaran, Bay Islands

EL SALVADOR — PIPIL, Quelepa, Tazumal

NICARAGUA — NICARAO, Ometepe Is., Rivas

COSTA RICA — Nicoya, Filadelfia, Las Mercedes, GUETAR, Chiriqui, CHOROTEGA

PANAMA — Gaucamayo, Venado Beach, Parita, Cocle, Veraguas, Chiriqui

WEST INDIES — CIBONEY, CARIB, TAINO, Lucayo, ARAWAK

[29]

KINGS, EMPERORS AND CACIQUES

The Truly Pre-Columbian World

Certain ground rules will be helpful in this consideration of Middle American aesthetics. First of all, it is simply for contemporary convenience that I have elected to proceed from north to south. Ancient man traveled in every direction, trading far and wide; we are now certain that much of his early journeying was also from the south. But if we were to do the same in our examination of his arts, the result would only be to confuse. Forthermore, early man was not conscious of our latitudes, longitudes and political boundaries. The borders which he cautiously observed had to do with natural barriers or the frontier limitations established ¡by powerful chieftains of the time. These he respected, or placed his head in jeopardy.

For the purposes of this volume, and to achieve a measure of order, we shall move from northern Mexico south through the Isthmus of Panama, and then to the West Indies, treating the various regions by their contemporary political designations, realizing as we do that this treatment violates most early concepts of space and habitation.

While a definite effort has been made to consider every major region, it will be at once evident that some fare less well than others. This is not to say that these had no art; it may simply be that we know less about the area, that perhaps the arts were of a perishable nature, or they may have been less in evidence . . . . or it may only be that other regions overwhelm our attention. For, as we shall see, some peoples made much more dramatic use of their resources than others. Perhaps they enjoyed a happy combination of temperament, environment, location and social development which permitted such supremacy. All of these have a bearing upon artistic success, for it is rare that great art comes from sparse resources and impoverished economies—and isolated folk often lose that inspiration which can come from frequent contact with outside forces. Thus, it is only to be expected that those who lived in the hub of active trade routes, and profited economically by that location, should also benefit culturally.

If there seems a degree of under emphasis of the massive works for which some of the Middle American cultures are justly famed, it is not to deny their majesty. It is simply that these great sculptured stelae, imposing stone monuments and magnificent architectural triumphs have been considered in great detail in many volumes. Many of these sculptures are less aesthetic than gross, and I believe that insufficient attention has been given some less pretentious but equally remarkable regions due to this preoccupation with large-scale art.

And finally, in each of the sections which follow, we are forced to base any conclusions we make upon only the arts which have survived; while regretting this imbalance, we cannot discuss " what might have been " with very much profit.

The Northern Deserts

We know little of the prehistory of this whole northern region of Mexico; it is certain that wandering hunters once existed here, although apparently not in great numbers. They were not late-comers, and we can fairly confidently place them in Sonora, Chihuahua and Coahuila as early as *circa* 10,000 B.C., when primitive cave-dwelling people briefly settled in the region and left flint-chipped tools in their wake. Of their arts, we know nothing.

Very slowly, the northern pioneers developed urban centers, became quasi-permanent settlers, learned how to make pottery, and became acquainted with neighbors to the north in southwestern United States (they may have been distantly related). By about A. D. 1000 a socially structured civilization was in being; the great center at Casas Grandes was surging toward its peak. Apparently intruders forced these people to band together for protection, agriculture became more systematic, and an extended trade brought about increasing expansion of this village core.

As merchants fanned out into the southwestern United States, contacts with the Anasazi folk increased; the earlier Mogollón and Hohokám influences continued, and urbanization increased. But another influence had made its appearance—Toltec and Tarascan merchants established trade relations which were followed by increasing political interest; eventually such centers as Casas Grandes seem to have become great population centers in which economics played a major part. Lines of communication expanded, bringing knowledge of new raw materials, new manufactured articles, and—of far greater importance—new ideas. Much of this is reflected in the recent work of Di Peso at Casas Grandes. At its height, the ceramics from this cultural center is equal to anything produced in late Pueblo times, and for range of imaginative design, ceramic quality and aesthetic beauty, holds up well among all Mexican pottery (Plates 2 and 3).

Later, the Aztecs expanded to the north, and while we are not yet fully acquainted with the results of this encroachment, we know that it made itself felt in the arts. The Quetzalcóatl cult, use of ball courts, casting of metal, and other techniques came into the culture; but perhaps the greatest effect of this " opening up " was the avenue it provided for Spanish slavers and gold-seekers after 1521.

Farther to the west in Sonora, we know less, for no great cities were built. With few resources to support a large population, this continued to be an isolated region of scattered hunter folk eking out a meager subsistence. No major ruins have been encountered in these vast desert tracts; this very fact may be the reason that these people escaped the eradicating trinity of disease, soldier-slaver and missionary, which so completely destroyed most of the other groups. Surprisingly, the more primitive civilizations of Mexico have fared better than the higher cultures in the effort to survive the advent of the White man. A remnant of this intermediary period is perhaps represented by the graceful clay figure in Plate 1. Attributed to the Seri, who inhabit Kino Bay today, it is impossible to date accurately, since the land surface is subjected to extensive natural change from year to year. The identification seems logical, for the Seri claim to recognize these figurines, although they remain comfortably vague as to their function. The conical head form is suggestive of the archaic " gingerbread figures " of the Jalisco-Colima-Nayarit region, which also feature sharply pointed triangular heads. Caches of as many as ten of these have been found, carefully arranged in a circle, as though at a shrine. The remarkably simple, effective design is not unlike the Cycladic figurines from ancient Greece.

Excavations in southern Sonora and neighboring Sinaloa, primarily by Ekholm and Kelly, have revealed centers of considerable habitation, with pottery of a quality indicating the presence of well-developed cultures whose extent is yet to be completely detailed.

Peoples of the Pacific

This rich area, at once the most familiar, yet least known major archaeological region of Mexico, has been exploited for decades. From it comes the smooth, rounded clay *techichi*, the little mute dogs fattened for food; the diseased effigies; the grotesquely ornamented figurines and the masterfully modeled genre forms all so popular in "Primitive Art" circles. Encompassing roughly the area from Río Mezquital to Río Balsas, the influences spread from the state of Nayarit through Jalisco and Colima into neighboring Michoacán. The term " Tarascan," frequently applied to the creators of these fantastic clay objects, is confusing, since there is no concrete evidence that they are related to the present-day Tarascan people, other than by geographical concidence; yet we have no better name to apply.

Unfortunately, almost none of this art has been excavated under controlled circumstances; most of it has come from old collections, long out of the ground, and without satisfactory data—or from professional *huaqueros*, men who make a living by looting tombs. These latter are not only untrained in the scientific values of archaeological preservation, but are also unwilling to reveal the sources of their digging, for fear of competition from rivals, or entanglement in legal difficulties. In each of the states involved in this section, less than a half-dozen excavations have been undertaken by qualified scholars. This is not due to neglect on the part of the student; the western Mexican region has long been isolated and somewhat hostile to outside penetration, and other regions have claimed the major share of formal archaeological attention.

But this lack of control does mean that our knowledge concerning the cultural background of this wonderful artistry is remarkably scant, in view of the vast quantity of recovered material. It is possibly true that more unbroken clay *objets d'art* have been extracted from the tombs of western Mexico than any comparable region; in most other sections of the country, earth movement or other factors usually mean that the material is recovered in damaged condition and must be restored later. While this record of unblemished recovery may be a tribute to the skill of the unlettered *huaquero*, it is a tragedy to Mexican science, for such huge numbers, excavated under scholarly conditions, would certainly have yielded equally rich stores of information.

These people left behind them a bizarre stage upon which literally thousands of actors promenaded, dressed in amazing costumes. What their rôles were, we can only guess; but nowhere in Middle America does there seem to have been such a rich profusion of plastic variation in design. The only possible rivals would be in the Valley of Mexico, and perhaps Veracruz. Clay figurines south of these regions tend to be subject to a much more rigid stylization.

The characteristic ware is a coarse-grained, reddish clay which smooths to a plain surface finished off by painting (Plate 7). There is also a buffware, found most frequently in Colima (Plate 13). In Nayarit, the art of the grotesque had its apogee. Here were brightly painted clay figures, costumed in painted textiles, wearing enormous loads of jewelry—ornate nose rings and ear whorls; odd (to us) headdresses; a wide variety of accessories—all busily engaged in daily activities. Some warriors are in battle array, others are posed as if for a portrait. These figures are often found buried in pairs in tombs—perhaps a man and wife together (Plates 4 and 5). But the forms and faces also occasionally suggest diseased persons—or mayhap an attempt at humorous caricature. Small house-groups are often found, with several tiny residents " at home "; amorous couples, brawling drunks and jaunty dancers enliven the otherwise static sculpture.

A similar situation obtains in Jalisco, but perhaps less exuberantly. One is inclined to suspect that the Jalisco folk felt secretly ashamed of their undisciplined countrymen who never seemed to settle down to more sober activities. Thus, they expressed their feelings in more ponderous creations, as they sat and brooded over their erring neighbors. There is less of the happy-go-lucky feeling about Jalisco art; the stolid, staring faces seem to indicate a more staid bourgeoisie.

But it was in the compact Colima region that solidity, exuberance, and dramatic depth find their greatest outlet. Here, one will see anything: humor, anger, pomp, tragedy ... whatever the emotion, it can be found in the small world of Colima (Plate 95). Truly, here is a newspaper of the ancient world. What were the ancient people trying to say with these thousands of little clay figurines, too carefully made for children's toys, yet seemingly not intended as major art creations for presentation to kings? They are usually found buried in tombs, often in great numbers; was this an attempt to provide the deceased with a counterpart of the world he had just left? Were these servants intended for his future comfort? Or were they simply symbols of affection, interred as a last tribute? We will never know—but we will always be grateful for this range of genre art which adds so measurably to our knowledge of the life of the ancient Mexican Indian. This was certainly no casual activity; fully three-fourths of the modeled ware from western Mexico is concerned with this attempt to depict daily life, which forces us to the conclusion that there was a definite purpose behind all of this clay work. It is for this very reason that such arrangements as shown in Plate 100 are possible ... and it may just be that this was what the original creators of these charming objects had in mind.

In addition to this ability to reflect daily life in their ceramic artistry, the potters of Colima had a tremendous feeling for form. Many of their vessels have an almost voluptous, clean-lined quality which would be remarkable in any art expression; the bowl in Plate 14 displays this at its best.

The Great Heartland

The Central Plateau and adjacent Valley of Mexico has provided much of the material included in this volume. In one sense this was not the major source for the artistic expression of the Mexican folk, but it was always a core around which the peripheral peoples ranged. Varying with the times, this part of Mexico saw the birth, florescence and death of dozens of tribal groups; some left artistic master-works behind, while some passed with no traces but scattered footprints. But all contributed some influence, large or small, to the over-all ethos that is Mexico.

The Mysterious Olmec. Were these the " original Mexicans "? Theirs is the oldest full-blown civilization to which we have been able to attach a corporeal entity. There is certainly ample evidence of earlier human occupancy in Mexico; usually this period is termed " Formative," or " Archaic," depending upon the classification used. These earliest cultural horizons are largely indicated by varying quantities of bits and pieces showing human presence, but for the purposes of this volume, they rarely provide us with any examples of aesthetically significant material culture. They are primarily important in proving the existence of far earlier human occupancy than had heretofore been believed probable.

It now seems certain that the style which we know as Olmec had a long developmental period, rooted in this earlier Formative epoch. The classic form of Olmec art style is obviously the result of many years of perfection; the skills may have been learned through other design styles, of course, but certain peculiarities of drilling, incising, and the basic arrangements all seem unique and none of them is thechnically simple.

The most astonishing features of Olmec civilization are the remarkably widespread area over which it has been found, the tremendous quantity of examples recovered to date, and the uniformity of the features making it identifiable. Even so, we know almost nothing about the people who created the style. For it may just be that this was not a " culture," but simply an art style, fashionable for a period, but which passed with the eclipse of those who found it admirable for their purposes. Many epochs in world history have enjoyed just such an ephemeral existence, owing their birth and continuum solely to political, social, or religious needs, disappearing when they became redundant.

At any rate, there now seems little doubt that an Olmec tradition existed from *circa* 1000 B. C. to A. D. 100, enjoying a peak period around 250 B. C. Elements in this style continued well into the Christian era, of course; but this was apparently only as residual art forms, rather than as mirrors of a contemporary culture (in fact, these elements still find considerable expression in certain stone carving today, notably in the Taxco region of Guerrero).

The work of Stirling, Drucker and his associates, and the later studies of Covarrubias have contributed the most significantly to our understanding of Olmec art today. They have traced the various forms which make up the tradition, the relationships of the so-called " baby face " complex, the spread of the style, and have solidified the basic patterning first given discrete identity by Saville and Vaillant.

The characteristic jaguar-mouth, rounded facial form with obese features and heavy-lidded eyes, shown in Plates 26, 40, and 43, all manifest the presence of the Olmec artist. The extreme range of the art forms has made it extremely difficult to locate the cradle of these baby-faced sculptures. Present evidence points to the Gulf Coast, in Veracruz, as the probable region, whence it spread all through the Mexican Plateau as far west as the Pacific Coast, eastward into the Yucatán Peninsula, and south into Honduras, Guatemala and El Salvador. The profusion of Olmec material in Guerrero has led many authorities to consider this as a more likely more original heartland for these folk, but far too little controlled archaeological investigation has been done in the area to make any definite conclusions possible.

The art is marked by an abundance of masks and figurines which feature the jaguar-mouth design, clay pottery with sophisticated linear decoration incised on the surface, unusual " votive axes " (Plate 61), and most particularly, an ability to handle jade as though it were plastic. The incredible forms carved from rich green jade, drilled with microscopic holes, bespeak a rare technological skill coupled with a sensitive feeling for the forms inherent in the stone. The comparison, often suggested, allying Olmec with the Chavín civilization in ancient Peru takes on considerable validity if considered in such aesthetic and technological terms; when the temporal relationship is included, the suggestion seems even more striking.

Beauty in a Brickyard. The Nahuatl term, *taltilco,* which means " where things are hidden," has been applied to a locality near Mexico City long exploited as a source of clay for making bricks. Occasional figurines from here had appeared in museum collections for many years, some prior to 1900, but it was not until the greater exploitation of these brickyards was undertaken that the material sold to collectors began to interest archaeologists seriously. By 1942, when Covarrubias worked in the area, and somewhat later with the efforts of Porter, the real importance of the site became evident. Tlatilco yielded many objects which exhibited characteristics common to the Olmec folk: a wealth of clay figurines, faces with jaguar-mouths, a great use of masks, incised designs on pottery similar to Olmec work, and finally, a radiocarbon date indicating occupancy contemporary with those folk. Although no great finds of carved stone or extensive use of jade have been uncovered, there seems little doubt that the two cultures are related.

The fantastic " pretty ladies," familiar to most collectors, are found in great profusion at Tlatilco, and are among the loveliest examples of prehistoric art (Plate 33). Vaillant organized these into a range of types in an effort to classify them; although later finds have expanded the series, his classification remains standard. The mask complex, as represented by Plate 32, is present in many sizes and types, as is the excellent pottery (Plate 34). This latter includes bowls with stirrup spouts, incised designs suggestive of Olmec tradition, a fascination with form for its own sake—and most intriguing, a similarity to some pottery forms found in the southeastern United States. Tlatilco was the cumulation of the Zacatenco civilization, which lasted from *circa* 1500 B.C. until perhaps 250 A.D., and remains the best known site illustrative of that era.

As with the Olmec peoples, the inhabitants of Tlatilco remain a mysterious and exciting folk; their arts reveal the existence of a great cultural expression, replete with all that we have come to think of as manifesting a " higher civilization." And the very fact of their extreme antiquity makes them the more fascinating.

Flooded Glories of the Past. Just as Tlatilco seems to represent the major phase of the Zacatenco culture horizon, and by visual evidence an extension of the Olmec tradition, Chupícuaro is a high spot in the Ticomán epoch. This latter, perhaps a forerunner of what later came to be the great Teotihuacán civilization, existed from *circa* 500 B.C. until the Christian era. The most important site, Chupícuaro, is a cemetery on the border between Guanajuato and Michoacán, and is famous for its beautifully modeled figurines. These slant-eyed, round-breasted ladies, painted in bright colors and decorated with tiny pellets of clay, are found in great numbers (Plate 17). Although most are

completely nude, some wear elaborate costumes, many have tiny little " pompom " sandals, and all have intricately fashioned coiffures. Along with these attractive figurines is a fine redware, sometimes worked into figurines, but more often formed into beautiful globular bowls painted with black and cream geometric decorations (Plate 16). The highly polished surface and rich red color make these outstanding in any collection of Mexican ceramics.

Chupícuaro art is lacking in stone, bone or other materials; like Tlatilco, these were artists in clay, who prided themselves in this one medium, and seemingly practiced little else. There is little Olmec influence evident in Chupícuaro design, and were it not for the occasional jaguar-mouth figurines, and a few other scattered indications, one would be inclined to treat them as complete immigrants into the Olmec region. But there does seem to be sufficient remnant usages to consider these as part of the long Olmec sequence. There is also ample evidence that the world was changing.

As in most Mexican figurine art, the earliest " archaic " forms are modeled of solid clay, with decorations added by painting, incising, or appliqué. With later and increased skill, these give way to hollow work, still modeled by hand, also decorated by painting, incising, or the application of tiny bits of clay. These hollow-ware pieces are usually aesthetically the most satisfying, normally indicating the classic period of the given culture. The earlier Chupícuaro figurines are modeled relatively crudely in solid clay, with elongated legs. The later, and technically more finished, clay work is based upon proportions almost exactly reversed from the Tlatilco stylization: whereas the pretty little Chupícuaro girls have slender legs and hips with large, rounded breasts suspended from wide shoulders, the prevailing ideal of feminine beauty at Tlatilco was apparently the narrow-shouldered, small-breasted woman, with tiny hips and huge, flaring thighs. To us today, both are equally charming, each in her own way.

Although a considerable amount of serious excavation has been accomplished at Chupícuaro, notably by Porter, there is little promise of further basic data, other than that which can be secured from museum collections. With the completion of the Solís Dam on the Río Lerma, the cemetery has been flooded, and the site is now lost to archaeological investigation. As at Tlatilco, where the brickmaking process has destroyed the whole complex, any further information gained will be meager. But this is not a unique threat in

Middle America; a similar fate awaits many of these smaller archaeological sites, however rich their potential. Only those large enough to attract tourist interest can hope to gain the attention necessary to insure their preservation.

The Home of the Gods.   As the Aztec name indicates, Teotihuacán is where the gods were believed to have lived. However, this great site was actually in ruins for several centuries before the Aztecs arrived; we do not know who constructed this tremendous metropolis. With an area of some seven square miles, it is by far the largest man-made construction in ancient America, being twice as extensive as either Tikal or Chichén Itzá, the next in size. Furthermore, it should be remembered that all of this was accomplished long before the introduction of metal tools into Middle America. Present dating regards the Teotihuacán period as including four major divisions, extending from about 250 B.C. to approximately A.D. 650. Most of the building work was undertaken by Indians who were still Stone Age Americans; size, as such, held no fears for the early builders of Middle America.

The architecture and city-planning arts of this epoch have been admirably covered by Marquina, and more recently by Kubler; hence I have chosen to concentrate upon some of those arts which, though lesser in dimension, may prove more comprehensible in scope.

The characteristic Teotihuacán " symbol," if such there be, is the carved stone mask, usually of a green stone, which has come to be identified with the site and the culture (Plate 42). Yet, as the present example demonstrates, these have been found throughout Mexico—thus providing at the same time a symbol of the widespread influence of this urban center. Almost none of these finely carved masks are accompanied by adequate provenience information. They have long been the target of the *huaquero*, the staple item of the dealer's stock, and the prize of the collector . . . and probably no other single object has been the subject for as much fraudulent imitation.

The traditional Teotihuacán figurine is the type illustrated in Plate 21. Like so many " traditional designs," these are found in many sizes, from 2 inches to 12 inches in height, all reflecting essentially the same form. They are usually carved from a dark green stone, and the purposes for so many sizes are unknown; probably they are based upon economic factors. The facial design is repeated in the painted clay maskette in Plate 27; other equally typical figurines in clay are of the type shown in Plate 28. A less stylized design, representing a decadent period in the later Teotihuahán epoch, is the aberrant *brasero* in Plate 35; the major interest it holds for us is the detailed iconography relating to the god Quetzalcóatl.

It is of equal significance that influence can be a two-way street; the covered effigy jar in Plate 38 is certainly evidence of contact between Teotihuacán and Kaminaljuyú. Although we are certain this originated in the south, we cannot know whether this was traded north peaceably or was brought back as booty. Of one thing we can be certain: at its maximum extension, Teotihuacán was one of the major forces in Middle America, spreading its culture from southwestern United States well into Guatemala, exerting a socio-economic influence not unlike that of New York, London or Paris today. In this, it was rivaled only by the Aztecs and Mayans, each of whom covered a somewhat similar geographical range.

Sometime around A.D. 650 or shortly before, Teotihuacán was destroyed. Its magnificence had long since departed with the decline in importance of this ceremonial center, but what was left was buried in tombs, under rubble, or carted away by the invaders. We know of this great civilization primarily by museum collections, the huge pyramid zone just outside of Mexico, City and the ubiquitous objects which show up all over Middle America, bearing evidence of its influence.

The Wanderers of Tula.   Just who the conquerors were, we are not sure; most evidence points to a Nahuatl-speaking peoples called the Toltec. This gifted warrior group was never numerically very large, apparently, but it was exceptionally efficient. We do not even know where the Toltec originated, but by A.D. 900 they were well-known in the Valley of Mexico. Soon they had developed a central " capital " at Tula, and extended their sway as far distant as Chichén Itzá.

The Toltec were among the earliest people in central Mexico to make use of metal, probably obtaining it from Central America by trade. Their art is not graceful; it features a static line, deeply carved sculpture making great use of shadows, but lacking in subtlety; there is a certain stiffness which makes it somewhat harsh. Many Mayan influences are exhibited in Toltec aesthetics, and though theirs was an extremely short-lived era, yielding to the

Chichimec and later Aztecs by A. D. 1200, they left an impress far out of proportion to their time.

Contemporary with the rise of the Toltec, another center developed—Xochicalco, the " place of the flowers " (Plate 36). This ceremonial structure in Morelos represents the northwest frontier of the then-expanding Mayan culture; it may have been the northern terminus for a Mayan trade route through Guerrero, along the Pacific Coast. This would account for many of the puzzling objects which have been discovered in that western section of Mexico, for we know far too little about the interrelationships of the coastal parts of Guerrero and Oaxaca. Variations as extreme as those in Plates 39 through 43, all found within a relatively limited area, indicate a considerable degree of cultural exchange; the problem is to decide which, if any, was the primary form, native to that particular area.

In Guerrero, evidence has been found of a mysterious culture, or perhaps simply an art form, which Covarrubias named *Mezcala*, after the river by that name. Who these people were, precisely when they lived, and where, we are not certain. But they left astonishing examples of abstract art behind them, notably the carved stone figurines based upon the lines of the utilitarian celt, in which a few basic cuts created human forms in the simplest manner imaginable (Plate 39).

East of the Sun. Life was stirring in this Gulf Coast region of Mexico as early as 1500 B. C., but the aesthetic expressions which concern us did not begin to make themselves apparent until about 500 B. C. By then, a group of Mayan folk, called the Huástec, had become separated from the parent body and settled in the Pánuco region of Veracruz. Apparently the force which cut them off was composed of Totonac settlers who were in process of building up their own major center at Tajín.

At this same time, or perhaps slightly earlier, the Olmec peoples were occupying another outpost, busily engaged in the manufacture of the great stone heads found by Stirling at La Venta and Tres Zapotes. These colossal carvings, so reminiscent of present-day football players, only increase the mystery which surrounds this group. And finally, Teotihuacán was energetically collecting the tons of earth fill, stone facing and other material to create the massive Pyramid of the Sun—prelude to making itself felt all through the eastern shores of Mexico.

This interrelationship of apparently unrelated peoples in Veracruz has been the source of great confusion. Each was a major expression in its own right, each left an indelible impress upon the region, and each apparently knew something of the other—and occasionally included that awareness in its art. Add to this the usual difficulty in obtaining archaeological provenience for the more critical objects existing today, and the reasons for our difficulty in establishing identities, boundaries, and specific chronologies becomes quite evident.

That we are dealing with major art expressions is ably demonstrated by the massive stone figure in Plate 76; this classic work shows Huástec sculpture in its most powerful form, for it is exceeded in grace only by the famous stone " Adolescent " from Tamuín, reproduced in almost every study of Mexican art. The clay figurines of the Huástec are not too greatly different from the larger Tlatilco figurines; usually made in creamware, the rounded modeling suggests considerable Olmec influence. Another puzzling form, limited to the Huástec area, are the carved shell gorgets whose designs are so suggestive of Mixtec art (Plates 74, 46).

By and large, these Pánuco artist were a somber lot, creating staring, static works only occasionally relieved by touches of liveliness. It is to the Totonac modelers we must turn to find any parallel with the exuberant imagination, realism and humor so common to the western part of Mexico. The innumerable "laughing faces," wearing various types of headdresses—some vacuous, staring effigies, some obviously happy-go-lucky gamins (Plate 64); the majestic matron with a fan (Plate 70); the gaily swinging girls, each a whistle, each tuned differently (Plate 71)—these all show various aspects of early Totonac life. The priest in an elaborate costume (Plate 66) contrasts vividly with the simply-modeled head of a lovely young girl (Plate 63). All of these reflect the life of the folk, unlike the neighboring Huástec to the north.

Many of these, like the swinging girls, are musical instruments; the latter are representative of literally thousands of clay *pitos* which have been recovered from burials (Plate 81). Usually these whistles are much less elaborate, but they are distributed throughout the region from northern Mexico to Panama; indeed, they are even more numerous in the south. Like the clay work of Colima and Nayarit, these often reflect the activities of the country people, and are as valuable for contemporary scholars. Large numbers of clay rattles have also been excavated; these hollow figurines, filled with pebbles, also depict customs and costumes of the day. Although their use is not definitely established, they may have had a religious or secular use, and quite probably enjoyed a dual rôle. One can readily imagine small boys of the period walking along the streets of their village, tooting on such clay whistles or keeping time with small clay rattles; this was a musical world, indeed.

Unique to the Gulf Coast is the use of native asphalt, *chapopote,* to add a touch of color to clay sculpture. The pools of oil welling up out of the ground provided a natural resource which early artists utilized in many ways (Plate 70). Occasionally these figures are found coated solidly with this black asphalt covering; on other types, white clay is often rubbed into the buffware design for contrast. A red-painted polished ware, most common to the region around El Faisán, has become diagnostic of one type of Veracruz ceramics (Plate 71).

Perhaps the most characteristic form of Veracruz art is the great variety of buffware clay figurines showing what are presumably ceremonial activities—the great wealth of costuming, elaboration of design and ornamentation—from which we can gain such a great amount of information concerning the early life of these people (Plate 69). The grotesque often combines with sculptures of considerable physical size to contrast strongly with miniature forms, all sensitively proportioned to hold scale in any size (Plate 68). Some of this sculptural work is as delicate as anything yet found in Mexico (Plate 72).

A short distance off the Veracruz coast is the small Isla de Sacrificios, a ceremonial center and cemetery from which hundreds of objects have been recovered over the past three centuries. Most notable of these treasures are the "alabaster" bowls carved in various animal and human forms (Plate 67). A buffware pottery, painted in strong designs, is also common to the island (Plate 62).

It is also in this part of Mexico that the most puzzling stone artifacts are found. Although the *palma,* the *hacha,* and the *yugo* are distributed throughout Middle America from central Mexico into El Salvador, it seems that their "birthplace" is here in the coastal Veracruz region. Certainly their numbers would indicate this. And while some of the most aesthetically pleasing examples of *hacha* sculpture are found in Guatemala (Plate 108), equally fine specimens are Mexican (Plate 60). The most intricately worked were produced by the sculptors at El Tajín (Plates 73, 75); these larger carvings show a wealth of detail in the style characteristic of that period and area. Smaller *palmas* are usually simpler in design (Plate 68). Numerically among the most common forms of Mexican stone art, we do not really know just what their function was. Of many theories advanced concerning their use, that of Ekholm seems the most reasonable to date, *i.e.*: their incorporation into the ball game as insignia; yet other arguments are also advanced. In spite of their relatively frequent occurence, they remain the most fascinating of early American stone sculptures, and the most mysterious.

The names come from early attempts to suggest usage: the *palma,* or "palmate stone," as it was called, was thought to have a religious role, while the thin-bladed *hacha,* or "ax," was so called from its fancied resemblance to an ax blade. Indeed, some suggestions were that it was a ceremonial symbol of the sacrificial ax. Lastly, the *yugo,* or "yoke," was thought to have been used as a weight to hold down the head and neck of a victim at the time of sacrifice. Today, none of these romantic theories are given credence, in spite of our inability to substantially prove otherwise.

The People of the Clouds. As early as 200 B.C., the Zapotec folk settled in the upland area dominating the Valley of Oaxaca, building one of the major civilizations of ancient Mexico. During their pre-eminency they constructed the great ceremonial complex at Monte Albán, one of the most picturesque of prehistoric American sites (Plate 49). Few other ruins present such a readily-understood sense of what the early Indian designer was attempting to accomplish in his use of space and architectural layout.

The Zapotec are best known for the magnificent modeled funerary urns which were placed in the vaulted tombs; these have been found in great numbers throughout Oaxaca. Bearing designs representative of important personages or deities in the Zapotec pantheon, these carefully worked sculptures tell us a great deal about the physical features of the people and their costuming. Few artists have as successfully mastered the formation of wet clay, or have as thoroughly explored the possibilities of ceramic elaboration. The early forms are more concerned with portraiture, while later work favors symbols indicative of status (Plate 51). The Zapotec civilization flourished for some ten centuries, yielding to the warlike Mixtec; these latter peoples moved into the region and by about 750 A.D. settled there, eventually combining forces to withstand the ever-increasing pressure of the Aztecs.

The Mixtec, " People of the Cloud Country," although recognized masters of many arts, were notable more for their technical wizardry than for outstanding aesthetic creativity. The intricacy of the turquoise mosaic shield in Plate 46 reveals the patience and incredible skill of these early craftsmen, and the gold jewelry in Plates 54 and 55 dramatically demonstrates their love for filigree. A form of pictographic communication was a Mixtec accomplishment; the *lienzo* in Plate 30 shows the visual form of this " writing." It continued into the Spanish period, by which time the Aztecs had adapted it to their own needs; however, this system is different from the hieroglyphic communication of the Mayans.

Almost unrecognizable today, the great pyramid of Cholula, in Puebla, was the center of the Mixtec world. This, the greatest man-made structure of ancient times, considerably exceeded the better-known Egyptian pyramid at Gizeh in size. In use at the time of the Conquest, the Spaniards destroyed much of it, using many of the structural blocks to build La Iglesia de Nuestra Señora de los Remedios, the church which now stands on the platform once graced by the huge stone statue of *Chiconahuiquiáuitl,* a rain deity.

Mixtec pottery is quite different from Zapotec clay art, usually featuring painted designs in place of the modeled work of the latter (Plate 45). Surprisingly enough, these artisans never mastered jade carving; of all the arts this seems least effective (Plate 52). Compared with the fine jade creations of the Maya, this is indifferent art, indeed.

Children of the Sun. As the barbarian hordes overran Europe, so did the Chichimec nomads under Xólotl raze such great cities as Tula and Culhuacán, and around 1200 A.D. established themselves supreme for a time in the Valley of Mexico. Accompanying them were a remnant band of mercenary warriors, originally insignificant, but who in time created the Aztec " empire." Calling themselves the *Mexica,* whence the name Mexico, they seem to have been considered more as pests than as outstanding warriors. However, their sudden attacks and merciless savagery soon gained them complete control over the Central Valley, and eventually almost all of Mexico. This very trait of unbridled cruelty led to their undoing, for subject tribes willingly coöperat-

ed with the *Conquistadores* to overthrow their hated overlords.

Aztec art is not subtle, and much of it is powerful but not particularly graceful. The favored medium was stone, which the artist carved in strong, dynamic designs (Plate 22). The brilliant Mexican sunlight dramatically emphasized the deep cutting and heavy shadowing of the work; the addition of solid areas of paint, while perhaps objectionable to contemporary taste, only increased that contrast. Medium-relief and bizarre combinations of form are common, often expressed in monumental terms—one carving, of The Water Goddess, still lies half-buried and unfinished, possibly because the carvers lacked the power required to extricate this huge stone mass from the base and to place it in position; or more likely, because of the Spanish invasion.

The most remarkable factor in Aztec sculpture is the tremendous quantity which has been found. Apparently this was a period wherein artists exploded in a veritable frenzy of activity. A favorite technique was the creation of dozens of similar statues, intended for placement along the avenues leading up to the temples, much as was customary in ancient Egypt. These statues were designed to hold banners or " standards " fastened to wooden poles (Plate 21). The well-known Aztec custom of human sacrifice is represented in the macabre preoccupation with skulls, severed hands, hearts, and other portions of the human body.

Pottery is at best only fair (Plate 31); Aztec craftsmanship in clay lacked the smooth quality so frequently seen elsewhere in Middle America. It seems more likely to provide a mirror for that vibrant power so evident in the Aztec world. Figurines appear to have lost the delicacy which characterizes earlier Mexican modeling, and the elaborate, but harsh, *braseros* in pottery lack any feeling of real sensitivity. Aztec writing, apparently an outgrowth of Mixtec pictographic communication, is somewhat like contemporary cartoon art; it is marked by strong outlines, with solid areas of contrasting colors.

In retrospect, one is impressed by a surge of stone art during the Aztec period, suggesting that other arts did not enjoy a similar degree of popular appeal at the time. Certainly, sculpture seems to represent the medium at which the Aztec civilization shows off to best advantage; just as one tends to think of goldsmithing or mosaic work as being a Mixtec speciality, or clay funerary urns as the Zapotec hallmark, most representative of that civilization.

Astronomers of Yucatán. In the vast plains of this eastern peninsular region, two major cultures vied for a time: the Toltec migrants from Tula, and the northern range of the Mayan people. The artistry of each is found scattered all through Yucatán, Campeche, Tabasco and Quintana Roo.

The most familiar Toltec site in Yucatán is Chichén Itzá; aside from certain elements reflecting Mayan influence, the basic pattern and architectural organization is clearly Toltec. The subsequent downfall of the Toltec civilization apparently brought Yucatán to a cultural standstill from which it never recovered; such mixed-motif objects as the mural at Tulum (Plate 92), and the various cave findings at Balancanché (Plate 93) only emphasize this range.

Surprising numbers of deer roamed this seemingly bleak area, supporting many colonies of people who raised corn in the *milpa* style, built temples which continue to turn up as archaeological research expands, and remain to puzzle the scholar with the oddments left behind. Such sites as Labná, Uxmal, Kabah and Mayapán demonstrate this problem (Plates 90, 91).

Just off the coast of Campeche is the Mayan island cemetery of Jaina, while adjacent to this on the mainland, is the more recently located site of Guaymil. In both areas some of the most sensitively modeled clay objects in Middle America have been recovered (Plates 80-85). Unfortunately, little of this material has been excavated by scholars; as is true throughout Middle America, most of these come from tombs looted by *huaqueros,* and any information concerning their provenience is largely circumstantial. But the careful modeling of the faces and the details of costuming provide some of our best information on the physical features and ethnology of these early peoples—and it is interesting to note that these are repeated time and again in the contemporary Mayan world.

The extension of this magnificent artistry into Chiapas and neighboring Tabasco proves this was not limited to the more eastern region. The magnificent wooden sculpture in Plate 87 not only overwhelms the viewer with its classic dignity, but it deepens our regret as we realize how many of these perishable masterpieces have been lost forever.

Not all Mayan art is delicate. Some is quite angular, some is not, as in the plumbate vessel in Plate 85; and some examples demonstrate a tremendous burst of power, as in the massive cylindrical urn in Plate 79. This introduces one of the architectural triumphs of Mexico—the magnificent temple site of Palenque, in southern Chiapas. Not only was this an outpost of the Olmec civilization (*e.g.,* Plate 78), but it was also a Mayan ceremonial center of major importance. The stucco head in Plate 77 is a further example of the unusually high degree of sculptural development reached by these people. The artistic expressions which were lavished upon Palenque represent the height of Mayan artistry, and are of a quality outstanding for any period in the history of human culture.

Highlands and Low. Although the Mayan civilization was a strong force in central and eastern Mexico, their heartland seems to have been somewhat farther south, in British Honduras, and particularly Guatemala. As early as 2000 B.C., and continuing up to about 300 A.D., this nuclear region gave rise to a cultural expression which reached its classic stage, surged forward in a great burst of energy, and collapsed by about 900 A.D. But during this period of classic greatness it represented a cultural level unequaled in Middle American prehistory. The art works which have survived reflect a greater feeling for aesthetic content, a consciousness of form, and an ability to exploit materials ranging from the hardest stone to the softest shell (even stucco was a favorite plastic medium), which only emphasizes their peerless position in American art. Some of the most remarkable architecture in Middle America emerged from this background, notably the spacious sites of Tikal, Copán, Quiriguá, Piedras Negras, and Uaxactún.

However, in spite of a wide range of art excellence, the Maya were never competent metalworkers. Very few pieces in gold, silver or copper have been recovered which can be identified as of Mayan origin, and of these, fewer still have any considerable aesthetic merit. This may in part have been due to the lack of metals in appreciable quantity in their homeland, but it does seem surprising that little seems to have been imported from distant metalworking centers.

Mayan art ranges from simple forms such as Plate 104 or 108 to such contorted and involved carvings as the stelae in Plates 114 and 138. Some designs show definite, distant relationships (Plate 117), while others provide the student with a considerable puzzle in efforts to identify origins (Plate 111). Not all Mayan work is smooth and sophisticated; however powerful it may be, the grotesque modeling of the fragment in Plate 100 seems crude indeed.

A peak achievement was in the field of jade working, in

which the Maya were rivaled only by the Olmec. An extremely difficult material to cut and polish, even by contemporary means, jade was highly prized by these early peoples; it held for them a quasi-religious importance, much as turquoise is regarded by Indians of the Southwestern United States. The work in Plates 58, 101 and 139 demonstrates not only the complete mastery of technique by the Mayan artisans, but also their love for the material. Other forms of jade carving were varieties of beads, ear flares, costume accessories, and dozens of types of decorative elements.

As did most other Middle America peoples, the Mayan artist added paint to his creation, even in outside architectural sculpture; unfortunately, the climate has removed most of this coloration. Only occasionally are we able to judge the original appearance of such works by the rare find which retains its color; those which have been recovered indicate a lively, if somewhat overwhelming, palette of natural pigment. Some indication of the original appearance of Mayan sculpture, with its painted designs, may be seen in Plate 86.

The most effective presentation of Mayan color sense is probably that manifested in polychrome pottery. Highly painted ceramics are to be found throughout the Mayan world, and Plates 88, 105, 137 and 140 demonstrate this as its best. This painting seems to have been most refined within the central Guatemala region; polychrome ware from Honduras suggests a bolder and somewhat less delicately painted design, perhaps due to contacts from Nicaragua and Costa Rica or possibly from Mexico.

Guatemala was also a great sculptural center, most particularly in such works as in Plate 121, and the unique figurine in Plate 113. Toward the Pacific Coast are the centers which produced the slender *hachas* (Plate 108), perhaps suggesting a penetration of Mexican cultural traits. While not unique to Guatemala, the interest in carving clay was most highly developed in the highland areas of that region, and Plate 107 illustrates one of the most characteristic forms of this ware, in which modeling is combined with forming. The unique vessel in Plate 120, while of uncertain date, reflects the strong design talents of the ceramic artists of this area.

Although centers such as Kaminaljuyú, Quiriguá, Holmul, and Uaxactún impress the viewer with their artistry, it is the grandiose layout of Tikal which literally takes the breath away. Here the tallest man-made structures of the New World are to be found, gracing one of the two or three most expansive urban-development areas of the Hemisphere

— proof indeed that the relatively short-statured Mayan people believed in the adage, " Think big, and stand tall."

In Honduras, the great ceremonial center at Copán represents a southerly extension of classic Mayan culture. Here, some of the most intricately carved stelae were erected (Plate 138), and some of the most powerful jade carving was undertaken (Plate 139). Along the valley of the Ulúa River, leading away from the eastern coast, is a cultural province which has yielded astonishing treasures in finely modeled clay figurines (Plate 141), together with painted ware (Plate 137). But of all artistic riches of Honduras, none are as famous, nor as intriguing, as the so-called "marble bowls" (actually a form of alabaster) found in a localized area in this Valley (Plate 136). Some have been found as trade objects elsewhere, but all seem to have originally come from this one center.

The Distant Frontiers. Evidence of contact between Mayan and non-Mayan folk is seen in many examples from Nicaragua, El Salvador, and Costa Rica. Here, the use of "glyph" designs on pottery is characteristic (Plates 124, 146, 153), yet this use was accompanied by a lack of understanding of just what these glyphs meant. This suggests either that artists were copying Mayan vessels, without a knowledge of the significance of the original—or else that these were people who had lost that knowledge, and were simply carrying on a past tradition, representing form without meaning.

The fact that the *yugo* and the *hacha* occur this far south is a further indication of extremely wide-ranging contact (Plate 128). The pyramid of Tazumal, with its great stone stela (Plate 132), is certainly related to those in Mexico and Guatemala, and the large carved shafts in Costa Rica and Panama (Plate 188) may carry on the stela concept, although it is more likely that they relate to similar shafts in South America.

Nevertheless, strong differences also exist in this area, suggesting that we are entering a peripheral point-of-contact between northern and southern Middle America. It is not a heartland for either culture, but one which fed from both, and seems not to have " jelled " into its own pure expression. Stone masks offer only a superficial resemblance to those farther north (Plate 130), and clay figurines are common, but again show dissimilarities (Plate 144). Yet the chocolate-ware vessel in Plate 145 presents a complete contrast to anything in Mexico, and the brilliantly painted figurine

(Plate 148) could never be mistaken for any pottery made farther north.

Almost all ancient art from El Salvador and Nicaragua betrays influence from neighboring areas; this will vary from piece to piece, and with the region involved. Many vessels found in El Salvador cannot be distinguished from work known to have been produced in Guatemala (Plate 123)—and the aesthetic creations of Nicaraguan artists often could have come from Costa Rica (Plate 148).

As with many other areas, this was a region of travel; even the sedentary cultures which developed were exposed to constant contact from the outside. Merchants and artisans carried their wares throughout the region, introducing ideas and knowledge. Many interesting and intriguing puzzles have been unearthed—we are not even sure where many of these folk came from, nor where they went. Much of this lack of knowledge is due simply to the fact so little arch-aeological work has been done; it is safe to say that fewer than a half-dozen professionally trained people have worked to any major extent in each of the three countries. Most of what we know is derived from looted sites or second-hand sources; only in very recent years has interest within the countries been aroused, and even this is quite limited in scope. This is a long-neglected area, and we pay the price of this neglect in ignorance. Yet careful and control-led excavation would reap tremendous rewards in the achievement of a greater understanding of New World migrations.

Ceramic artistry in Costa Rica is marked by strong motifs with bold color, usually in black and red-orange on a buffware base (Plate 158); some early period vessels in a polished redware with black decoration are also found (Plate 161). Although designs vary from heavy outlines to light tracings, and the thin-walled biscuitware is remarkable for its graceful delicacy, one tends to think of Chorotega and Nicoya wares as being powerful, solid-color styles. Modeling is not in the fine, detailed tradition so familiar to Mayan art; Costa Rican potters followed a more rounded form.

One interesting treatment, practiced in common with Panama artists, is the subtle use of modeling to emphasize painted decoration (Plate 158). While forms are usually quite simple, sophisticated examples are not infrequent, and show the hand of a master artist (Plate 156). South American influences, particularly in stone carving (Plate 167), seem to have worked their way up through Panama, and expended

themselves in Costa Rica, for they are rarely found north of this region.

Highway or Drawbridge? Of equal significance in the comprehension of Middle American prehistory is Panama. It cannot be dissociated from Costa Rica, nor can the neighboring section of Colombia be ignored; indeed, until 1904 it was a part of that nation. Again we must emphasize the point that arbitrary political designations often bear little relation to the boundaries recognized by the pre-Columbian citizens.

The people of this region were remnants of the parent Mayan group who were apparently isolated in early times, due largely to geography, and eventually developed a closer affinity with the Chibcha and Quimbaya Indians to the south. Their language indicates this relationship, just as it has also incorporated many Chibchan influences, and the various arts frequently betray kinship with both.

But the major design affilation is with Costa Rica, and a vast area extends from central Costa Rica to central Panama, in which essentially homogeneous art works continually show up. The pottery in Plate 160 and the gold in Plate 162 could have been found in either region. On the other hand, clay work from Veraguas of the type illustrated in Plates 168 and 179 would not be attributed to any other site. The pedestal bowl (Plate 186) is of a form found in many areas, but the decoration style would be seen nowhere else.

It is equally true that the use of gold is not unique to Panama or Costa Rica, yet certain individual motifs are seen which seem not to have occurred beyond the region; indeed, some forms are even confined to tightly restricted localities (Plate 182). In common with Colombia (where the technique may even have originated), the craftworkers of Costa Rica and Panama mastered the art of casting gold by the lost-wax process, and were able to create remarkable *objets d'art* whose beauty deeply impressed the Spaniards—who, it should be remembered, were familiar with the work of such artists as Cellini and Dürer. Indeed, Dürer entered in his diary an evaluation which has been quoted in almost every survey of pre-Columbian Mexican art:

> Also did I see the things which one brought to the King out of the new Golden Land ... all sorts of marvelous objects for human use which are much more beautiful to behold than things spoken of in fairy tales ... And in

all the days of my life I have seen nothing which so rejoiced my heart as these things. For I saw among them wondrous artful things and I marveled over the subtle genius of these men in strange countries.

These words, from one of Europe's greatest artists, followed his visit to the "Pre-Columbian Art Exhibition," held in Belgium in 1520. This display featured the treasures sent to Charles V by Hernando Cortés. After the several exhibitions, many of "these things" were presented to other European monarchs; the rest were melted down for their gold content, or their stones were removed for resetting in contemporary jewelry. Times have changed but little; as this is being written, verified accounts come to hand of a large cache of just such gold objects from Panama, looted by *huaqueros,* which were melted down in 1962.

While this strip of land may have served to link both Central and South America, it may well have been that the impassable jungle of Darién also may have proved a barrier to any prehistoric Pan-American highway. Archaeological evidence testifies to an equal, if not more important, sea route between the two regions. We may never know the whole answer to this riddle, but it is certain that proper excavation will yield some interesting evidence—and some surprises. Here again, almost nothing has been done under scientific conditions; in each country, a bare half-dozen scholars have worked against time in an effort to beat the gold-seekers to the tombs.

And plenty of evidence is to be found, for this was a well-populated region in which a great variety of art forms were combined with a remarkable aesthetic content. Furthermore, extreme antiquity can be demonstrated; radiocarbon dates as early as anything in Mexico or Guatemala have been recorded: *circa* 4850 B.C. at Cerro Mangote, and 2130 B.C. at Monagrillo. These promise rich returns in knowledge to the scholar, far greater than in many of the better-known sites in Middle America.

Island Sculptors. Least-known of all of the art areas included in this volume are those first encountered by Columbus. The people of the Antilles were divided into several linguistic groups with varying levels of cultural expression. The preëminent societies were the Arawak, Ciboney and Carib, each of whom included many subdivisions.

Of all of these, apparently the highest degree of artistic accomplishment was achieved by the Taino, a division of the Arawak, and who were most prominent in Puerto Rico, Hispaniola, and Cuba. Examination of any of the masterpieces in Plates 193, 198, 200 and 203 immediately reveals the power in their artistry. Since almost none of the perishable materials (textiles, wood or other "soft goods") has survived, we are forced to judge the Antillean aesthetic achievements in terms of stone or shell. Yet the very few wooden remnants extant offer ample proof of competency in that medium (Plate 208).

By far the most impressive quality in Taino art is the feeling for stone which these people held. Simple forms in outline have often only slight alteration to reveal a tremendous power (Plate 199); other examples indicate a complete altering of the basic stone to develop whatever concept was in the mind of the sculptor (Plate 198). At first glance, many objects seem gross and heavy; careful examination will show a smooth cutting with astonishing grace and strength (Plates 192, 203).

In clay, these artists were no less skilled; the outlines of the water bottle in Plate 194 are as effective as anything produced elsewhere in Middle America, and few pottery effigies are as remarkably eloquent as the dramatic crouching man in Plate 193.

The love for odd shapes by the inhabitants of the Lesser Antilles is fascinating (Plate 204, 206); these unusual objects are found scattered throughout the islands, and range from the most simple to quite complex designs.

The use of shell is seen everywhere; not only was this easy to work, but it was plentiful, and found ready acceptance as an art medium. Ranging from amusing and attractive objects such as those in Plate 191, through the more macabre types of decoration in Plate 197, all types of expression can be found. The long "swallow-sticks" are famous, but the more aesthetic *zemis,* or charms, have a greater appeal to contemporary eyes.

Though these islands held a large population, they were quickly stripped clean of human life, and aside from pockets of survival, in a short time the original inhabitants had been replaced by emigrants. Lacking any form of writing, losing their original identification so rapidly, they have left to us only these few mute records of their civilization. Almost no excavation has been conducted under controlled conditions, and of all of the regions considered in this volume, this vast area is by far the least known.

Nor will we ever really increase our knowledge in as great a proportion as in some of the other little-known regions of Middle America, for there are no widespread "ruins" to uncover. A few graves here and there, some undiscovered caves, and such sub-surface finds as may be encountered—these are the best that can be hoped for. By and large, those few large collections presently existing will have to supply the needed information, strengthened by such occasional discoveries as may come to light.

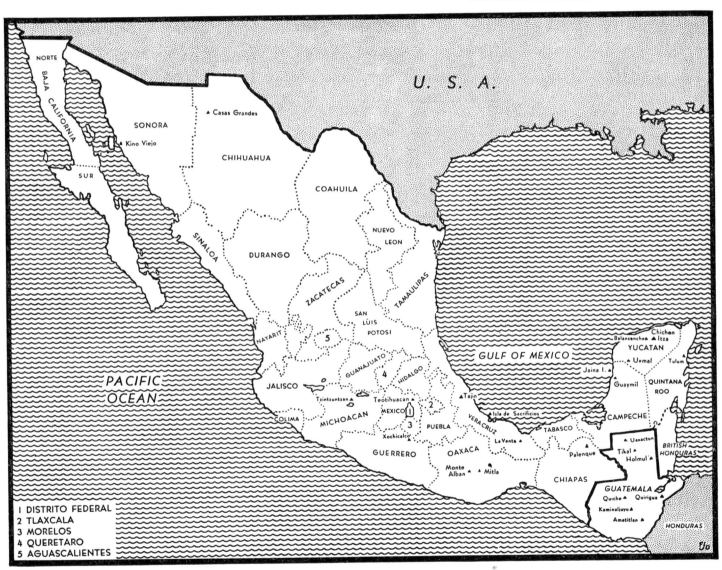

1 DISTRITO FEDERAL
2 TLAXCALA
3 MORELOS
4 QUERETARO
5 AGUASCALIENTES

WHEN THE WHITE GODS CAME

The legend of the return of the god Quetzacóatl and its incredible concidence for Hernán Cortés—with such tragic results for the pre-Columbian civilizations of the New World—has been recounted too often to require repetition here. The effects of this invasion upon the artistic achievements of the Indian were devastating for all time. The few beneficial factors can in no way offset the destruction of a whole social order, and the effects of this shock are demonstrated in the radical changes in Indian art which followed.

In the succeeding sections, our attention will be turned to those examples of Indian art created after the Spanish Conquest. In anthropological terms, all of these are regarded as *ethnological*, as opposed to the *archaeological* material considered in the previous pages. Although any object of this nature made after 1492 is technically post-Columbian, this " contact date " obviously varies from one region to another, since the *Conquistadores* did not invade nor overcome all areas simultaneously. For the purposes of this volume, the term *pre-Columbian* applies to material up until the very early years of the sixteenth century; specimens made after that date until the early nineteenth century fall within the *Colonial* era, and *Modern* covers the subsequent period until mid-twentieth century. Current, or very recent (within the last decade or so), manufacture should be regarded as *Contemporary* in chronology. None of these terms have any qualitative application whatsoever; a contemporary object can be as aesthetically successful as anything made a thousand years ago.

Smashing the Idols. Immediately following the Conquest, the self-righteous fanaticism of medieval clerics brought an abrupt end to much of pre-Columbian Indian art, most particularly those objects which the Spanish regarded as being idolatrous. Since a major amount of Indian art was of a religious nature, this meant the wholesale destruction of then-living art. Statues were smashed, wooden figures were thrown into the flames, clay effigies were broken up, and smaller pieces were buried, ground up as mortar, or otherwise disposed of. All gold and other precious materials were of course eagerly sought after and sent back to Spain.

Even more disastrous was the burning of whole libraries of books—the codices of the Mixtec, Aztec and Mayan scholars, in which was stored the accumulated knowledge of their world—knowledge at which we today can only hazard the vaguest guesses. This loss of recorded information far overshadows in importance the more frequently mentioned lust for gold which accounted for the disappearance of so many lovely *objets d'art*. And few Spaniards had the literary ability, or the inclination, to write down what they saw; only a few really worthwhile eye-witness reports on the life of the period are extant. These half-dozen or so remain our best sources for what little is known of the Indian civilization that flourished at the time of the Conquest.

With the change of political control, social organization underwent dramatic changes, and naturally the Indian artist was directly affected. He was no longer engaged in the creation of artistic objects for purposes which he understood; he had to produce things which had no values in his terms, and in many instances he was set to copying completely alien designs. The Spaniard had no use for, nor tolerance of, strictly Indian artistic concepts; he primarily wanted things around him which were somewhat familiar, or which at least reminded him of home. Thus he required the artisan to manufacture quasi-European items—that is, to copy them as closely as he could, minimizing the " Indian feeling " in design.

The result was a sharp drop in native expression, and art of the Colonial period in this region reflects this change very clearly. Although the artist was working with far more efficient iron tools, he rarely understood what he was copying—often with startling results, which are only occasionally aesthetically pleasing. Even more unfortunate is the ironic fact that this was a low period in Spanish art expression; thus the Indian artist, just lately arrived at a peak accomplishment, was set to imitating European art reflecting one of its worst epochs.

It is often assumed that the destruction of most of these Indian objects was due to the action of the Spaniard, either gold-seeker or priest, intent upon demolishing " the works of the Devil." While this certainly played a large part in such eradication of artistic work, two other agents were also responsible. The first was composed of invading alien Indian warriors, who obliterated many sculptures, particularly the larger stelae and major figures, in an effort to conquer and substitute their own religious and political hegemony. The second came at the hands of the indigenous folk themselves, in an occasional rebellion against their overlords.

Only small groups of Indians, living in isolated areas, managed to escape the Spanish vandalism; even fewer were able to withstand the alien Indian invasion. Thus we find that this man-made destruction was so thorough as to leave very little material above ground; rare indeed are the caches such as that found at Balancanché (Plate 93), or the miraculously preserved cave discovery illustrated in Plate 46. It is largely in tombs or graves that the records of past civilizations are to be found—and even here, the ravages of time, natural decay and chemical reactions, earth movement, or the carelessness of the *huaquero* have taken their toll.

GOLD, GRAVES AND SCHOLARS

To paraphrase a recent book title, these three have been major avenues in the achievement of an understanding of ancient civilizations. The first formed an impetus, the second provided raw resources, and the third gave interpretation. Other factors are often involved, of course—popular fashion, mentioned above; the accidental discovery of a site during construction work or natural phenomenon; exploitation in support of a particular theory, and so on..

The first two factors have remained fairly constant over the years, but a new voice has been added to the ranks of the third, which offers considerable promise in years to come. Just as the field of *ethnohistory* has so effectively assisted the field anthropologist in bringing historical documentation to bear upon legend and material culture, so can the art historian make a singular contribution in the efforts at unraveling and interpreting the early history of man in America. Trained in aesthetics, but keyed to the use of historical research tools, he can bring the eye of the artist into focus in synthesizing cultural development. In the past, true " art history " studies have been rare; in most research involving art expression, the attention of archaeologists has been largely directed toward a superficial examination of art style, and few individuals have been able to bring aesthetic evaluation into play in their investigations. This is not to criticize such studies as invalid, but simply to emphasize the opportunity present in this new field, which is available to students now in training.

Mid-century Miners. The day of the gold-seeker did not pass with the *Conquistador*. The story of the great loads of gold excavated in 1858-1859 in Chiriquí province, Panama, (then Colombia), and sent to the Bank of England to be subsequently melted down, is well known; among these shipments were not only badly damaged or corroded ornaments, but also *objects d'art* similar to those in Plates 164, 173 and 179. The haul was so great, in fact, that dentists advertised in newspaper ads that fillings incorporating archaeological gold were available. The gold rush which resulted from these finds led to little more than heightened fever; almost nothing of scientific value came from the frenzied digging in which almost the entire population engaged.

And the situation is no different today, as indicated by the frequent reports of large gold finds. Although the over-all numbers are smaller, aesthetically-significant gold ornaments are still being melted down solely for their metal content, or to escape detection and confiscation.

The point to this is simply, that to most scientists, gold represents the least welcome discovery in any archaeological excavation. It increases the danger of looting, outside interference, or possible violence—and above all, the loss of associated information concerning the circumstances of the discovery.

Subsidized Art History. In earlier times, the recovery of most art treasures was at the hands of rapacious armies, individual treasure seekers, or wealthy patrons. These latter ranged from men sincerely interested in scholarship and the arts, to *nouveau riche* persons solely concerned with establishing social status. As the princes of state or commerce found their mansions overflowing with such collections, quasi-public displays became customary. Eventually this led to full-fledged museums, operated in the public interest.

Such overt display required collecting on a more selective basis; knowledgeable scholars were brought in as advisers, and these patrons or their institutions undertook systematic exploration which laid the groundwork for a large proportion of contemporary archaeological investigation. These range from the half-century concentration of such collectors as George G. Heye and Robert Woods Bliss to those of David J. Guzmán and Miguel Covarrubias—and there are many, many others—all of whom have been responsible for the creation of outstanding public presentations of Middle American material.

Expeditions launched by such institutions as the American Museum of Natural History, the Museo Nacional de Guatemala, Peabody Museum at Harvard, the Instituto Nacional de Antropología e Historia (Mexico), or the Middle American Research Institute, have all made impressive contributions. Universities also entered Middle America in search of furthering artistic or anthropological knowledge, most notably those of Pennsylvania, Harvard, California, Yale, the Universidad Nacional Autónoma de México, and Mexico City College. Each of these has been responsible for an outstanding record of publications enriching our knowledge.

But it was with the forming of the great philanthropic foundations that some of the most significant work has been accomplished. The record is uneven, since the total number of anthropologically-oriented foundations is extremely small; but many general-interest organizations have supported such research as part of their over-all responsibility. Although the products of such field work are often displayed in art exhibits, by and large art museums have not taken part in such activity. Most of this sponsorship has been by way of anthropology, which accounts for the direction in which it has proceeded.

No operation of this nature approaches the remarkable accomplishments of the Carnegie Institution of Washington. Under the able guidance of Sylvanus Morley and Alfred V. Kidder, the excavation and reconstruction programs of such sites as Chichén Itzá, Uaxactún and Kaminaljuyú—to name but three of many—remain unequaled in scope, and are outstanding testimonials to responsible sponsorship of scholarly research. Until the program was terminated in 1960, the publications from this field activity provided the archaeologist with some of his most useful information.

Governmental participation in anthropological studies has long been active in varying degree, depending upon the political situation at the particular time. The establishment of the Bureau of American Ethnology by John Wesley Powell in 1879 resulted in many publications devoted to Amerindian art; many of the early titles were concerned wholly with Middle American areas, and even when attention became more confined to the United States proper, comparative studies of Indian art included a wide-ranging interest. The more recent establishment of the National Science Foundation has resulted in efforts to salvage archaeological sites before they are flooded by dams under construction, or by field studies of native cultures facing extinction. Even in the very short time this has been active, surprisingly successful results have been demonstrated.

Another sign of the future may be the joint collaboration of the Guatemalan Government (through the Museo Nacional de Guatemala) with the University of Pennsylvania, in excavating the ruins of Tikal. Such coöperative ventures seem certain to increase, particularly in those areas where such reconstruction will result in tourist attractions which can insure a long-time interest. As commercial organizations realize the very real advantages of funding such field excavation, this should become increasingly active in years to come; the excavation and reconstruction of Zaculeu, sponsored by the United Fruit Company, serves as a model of such enterprise.

As national pride increases interest in national culture, an appreciation of the values inherent in the indigenous background of the various areas will grow—as well as a protective concern for that background. From the use of stones from archaeological sites for construction material, or the destruction of historical structures to provide space for buildings, to the rapid acculturation of existing Indian minorities—and their arts and crafts—the problem of conservation is more and more apparent.

While it is unfortunately certain that all of these Indian cultures will eventually disappear, it is not necessarily inevitable that the knowledge of their artistic skills and techniques will be lost: this would be an inexcusable waste of human resources. The salvage of indigenous art proceeds in varying degree in the different regions. Some countries have established governmental agencies to effect this end (*e.g.,* the several *Indigenista* institutes in the Middle American region, and the U.S. Indian Arts and Crafts Board), while others have not yet become concerned. These latter have failed to realize the very real tourist-attraction values in economic terms, completely aside from the human elements involved.

Unlocking the Mysteries. Modern technological developments have provided the student with increasingly efficient equipment; the sensitive electronic "divining rod," used with such success by Stirling and Rainey, is one indication of these advances. Underwater archaeology using scuba apparatus opens up regions previously closed to exploration, and improvements in radiocarbon dating techniques combine to promise tremendous strides ahead in our search for

knowledge. Whether the highly touted use of computers will materially increase this knowledge is less certain at the present time.

The Mayan glyph system remains almost as great a mystery as ever, although breakthroughs from time to time, as new glyphs are discovered, enables us slowly to form new concepts. Dates continue to be pushed back further into prehistory with these discoveries, but complete decipherment, if it is ever to be accomplished, remains a long way off.

Perhaps the most promising development has been growing trend away from the somewhat sterile consideration of potsherds and taxonomy to the more fruitful collaboration of many academic disciplines. In this coöperative effort, the rôle of the arts is a major one, and the past few years have seen most productive results, with more certainly to come.

ARCHAEOLOGICAL SITES IN CENTRAL AMERICA

THE SURVIVING ARTS

The previous sections of this volume have been devoted to the aesthetic accomplishments of the Indian before the arrival of the White man. The following comments apply to Plates 209 through 248, all of which present the Indian arts of the very recent past. None of the specimens illustrated in those plates was created prior to ca. 1850, and some were made within the past five years. Thus they reflect the continuum of Indian art expression as practiced in Middle America today.

The selection has been based as much as possible upon Indian art forms; those expressions which seem to reflect predominantly European concepts fall more appropriately into the category of folk art. This arbitrary partition is intended to explore aesthetic survivals over the past 450 years of acculturation and to demonstrate those arts or regions where the residual qualities seem strongest. As in the archaeological section, it is not possible nor practical to attempt to consider every contemporary tribe; thus consideration is given only those which are most representative of each region.

One of the major historic differences between the survival of Indian art in North and in Middle America lies primarily in the fields of population and race relations. In North America, there were perhaps some 1,250,000 Indians scattered widely over the continent when the White man came; density was very slight, and such interracial contact as existed was rarely intimate. The White colonist or settler tended to kill off or to remove the Indian population to distant reservation areas; there were long periods of relative isolation,

and in some tribes the arts were not greatly affected. Later, when White migration into these areas developed, it came with a rush, and most of the Indian culture was precipitously erased; the few remnants were drastically altered.

In Middle America, the situation was rather different. Pre-contact population figures are extremely difficult to establish, for such early records as do exist tend to give exaggerated totals, usually in support of political or clerical claims. Educated guesses vary, but the consensus of estimates places the population of Mexico around 5,000,000 individuals at most, plus 1,000,000 for the balance of Central America. The West Indies probably did not number more than 500,000. By and large, these various groups settled in compact units, with high population density, leaving great uninhabited regions intervening between the settlements.

Of greater importance, however, was the fact that the Spaniard, in contrast to the English or French colonist, not only lived with the natives, but intermarried with them, and rarely practiced the custom of removing tribes to remote reservations. Thus, each absorbed some of the cultural patterns of the other, and, over a much longer period of assimilation, ideas and customs became imbedded in the native culture which are no longer readily identified. It is therefore vastly more difficult to particularize Indian art as an uninfluenced concept; arbitrary decisions are unavoidable.

And what is left of these contemporary patterns today? Just how many people are we talking about? The figures below will give the reader an idea of the population segment involved. Again, exact totals are difficult to obtain (in some countries Indias are no longer counted separately), but the most accurate estimates available are those provided in the *Indianist Yearbook* for 1962, published by the Inter-American Indian Institute.

Mexico	3,030,254
Guatemala	1,497,261
Honduras	107,800
El Salvador	100,000
Nicaragua	43,000
Costa Rica	8,000
Panama	62,187
Total	4,848,502

It must be pointed out that this does not include perhaps 250 individuals in Cuba, plus very small, scattered remnants in the Caribbean who have managed to retain a vestige of Indian culture. These latter would not exceed another 250. A glance at the accompanying map will show the distribution of the tribes in these countries, with their present population.

No effort has been made to include every tribe; only those involved with objects illustrated in the plates are considered.

The population estimates and tribal distribution tell us nothing more than how many Indian persons there are in the several Middle American countries. A majority of these would have no active connection with arts and crafts activities whatsoever; they would be farmers, urban laborers, or engaged in other non-art activities. And of those who do participate in the arts, many would be more accurately regarded as producers of folk art, rather than Indian art in the present sense of the term. This proportion would be higher in some countries, such as Mexico, than in others, such as Guatemala, where the indigenous art tradition maintains itself more effectively.

Color in the North. The Pelican People of the Sonora desert country lived originally on Tiburón Island, but were removed to the mainland in recent years. Today little remains of their former culture; the thin-walled pottery has almost

INDIAN TRIBES OF MIDDLE AMERICA

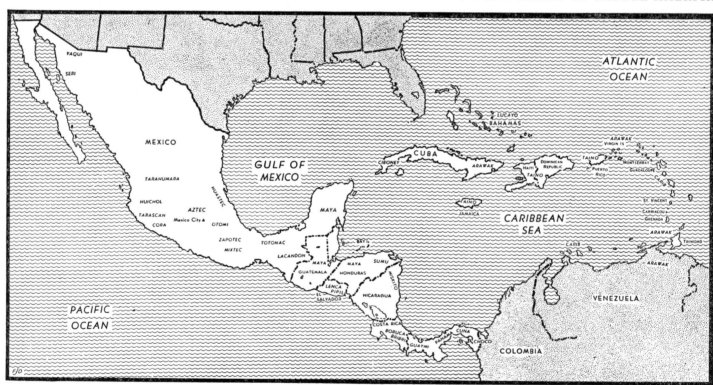

disappeared as a craft, and about all that is still being made is the *torote* basketry (Plates 209 and 210). Due to the encouragment of a few White visitors, the Seri women have begun a basket-weaving revival of sorts, but this may only be a temporary halt on the road to oblivion, for the function of the basket no longer exists, and there is no great demand for the type of coiled basketry they make. A striking art of earlier days was the remarkable body painting practiced by these Indians, customarily applied in linear or dotted patterns in white and blue paint.

Not far from the Seri are a group of related tribes, all speaking a Cáhita tongue, with several arts which have not lost their vigor. Perhaps most notable are the *Pascola* masks of the Mayo and the Yaqui (Plates 211 and 212). The Yaqui are particularly famed for their Deer Dance, a carry-over of ancient hunting rites; in this performance the use of silkworm cocoons for leg rattles has an interesting parallel. The same usage is found on clay figurines at Tlatilco, in costuming of two thousand years earlier (Plate 33, third figure from left). The other dominant art of the Cáhitan folk is in the textile field, particularly a wide range of belts and carrying-pouches (Plates 213 and 214). These latter are to be found all over Middle America, some plain, and some elaborately decorated (Plate 240).

Some of the most colorful ritual paraphernalia in contemporary art are the objects used by the Huichol of Jalisco and Nayarit. The eye-catching *sikuri* has become familiar to many tourists (Plate 215), even though these still are regularly used by the Indians in daily life. Another unusual art object is the votive bowl made from the calabash, tastefully decorated with a large variety of materials (Plate 216). The recent introduction of pictorial plaques in which realistic designs are worked with colored yarns, though quite charming, are due largely to outside inspiration.

Strangely enough, though the North American Indian excelled in beadwork, this craft does not seem to play an important part in Middle America. Even when glass beads are incorporated into costume details, there seems not to have been a comparable proficiency or taste in their use; the bracelet in Plate 217 is characteristic not only of the Huichol, but of several other tribes who also practice the craft. Only the Guaymí seem to have as much imagination in this art (Plate 237).

All of these folk live in relatively isolated areas; their contact with outsiders, though common, is sporadic. Many will spend months on end without seeing any but their fellow tribesmen; the country in which they live is difficult of access. But however sparse the region, they have developed a strong sense of color in their world. The vibrancy of the gourd bowl, the lovely softness of the God's Eye, or the strong design contrast in the belting is sufficient to demonstrate this fulfillment of man's need for beauty, no matter where he may be.

The Tarascan and Zacatec folk, two major groups in this region, reflect less of their pre-contact art styles than do some of the other smaller and more isolated tribes. They were exposed to immediate contact, and apparently were unable to retain as much of their independence; thus they are not included in the collection, even though they certainly produce some Indian art work. The indigenous quality seems less outstanding, and the motifs are largely of European origin; even in such pre-Columbian techniques as the famed lacquer ware of Uruapan, the only prehistoric element surviving in strength is the technical application of the lacquer itself; all else is more reflective of European than Indian culture.

Christo-Pagans; the Arts of Central Mexico. This term applies to a majority of the Indian peoples under consideration, but it is used here to indicate what might be called the heartland. For it was here in central Mexico that the earliest indications of ancient man in Middle America have been thus far discovered, and it was here that the White man first secured a permanent foothold. The bewildering complexity of pre-Columbian and contemporary art survivals blend in their maximum form—and are therefore least readily analyzed—in this region. As with most Indians, these tribes have taken on a surfacing of Christianity, while still retaining a remarkably strong degree of indigenous spiritual beliefs. The major non-Indian religious form introduced to them was Roman Catholic, which has developed in a manner particularly suited to Indian practice. Saints easily became gods; the great use of elaborately decorated vestments; altars and shrines; extensive introduction of figurines; incense; processions—all of this greatly aided the process of nominal conversion. In a sense, the Indian takes no chances; the ability of a polytheistic folk to adapt to new gods when the old gods fail is clearly evident. The customs, beliefs and practices all transfer over, and the new becomes a *mélange* with the old, presenting the ethnologist with a major headache. Some costume design elements can be readily traced to their European or Indian backgrounds, but many defy analysis. Usage, or timing, may or may not indicate pagan practice, for some seeming parallels are quite deceptive, since all peoples of the world observe certain rituals in common—the " rites of passage " of anthropological study, for example.

And as in religion, so in art; those who have accepted the most from the White man's religious practices likewise usually reflect the strongest alien art influence. Exceptions to this rule are rare.

In this area, the Otomí, the Mixtec and related Zapotec have kept several intriguing techniques thriving, while becoming everyday neighbors of non-Indians. The ancient art of paper-making by beating out the inner bark of the black mulberry is one example. Used in ancient times for the codices, it is employed today in the manufacture of cut-paper figures, used as offerings (Plate 219).

The textile arts were common in ancient Oaxaca, as recorded admiringly by the Spaniards; they remain so today. The strongly figured wool blankets so familiar to travelers are Indian in texture and weave, but the central motifs have undergone considerable change in reaction to non-Indian demand (Plate 220). The production of "Aztec Calendars," eagles perched on cactus plants, the lion of Castile, and so on, are perfectly respectable folk-art expressions, but they cannot be regarded as Indian art forms. The older *serape,* typical of a more northerly section, is frequently confused with the Oaxaca work, for these weaves were traded widely; many have been collected in the western part of the United States (Plate 222).

Throughout this whole area, the blend continues to puzzle the analyst. And, if it is any comfort, the native is often equally confused; varying legends will " explain " the origins of motifs, often in the face of visual evidence to the contrary. This discrepancy, while bewildering to the tourist, does not trouble the native to any degree.

And as these alien elements become part of contemporary life, they inevitably force out some motifs of aboriginal character. To some, this is a regrettable loss of " primitive charm;" to others, it is a gain in technical perfection. Unfortunately, it must be admitted that all too often technical skill wins out over good taste.

The major Middle American art loss is in the field of ceramic modeling; nothing is being produced today in this area which can compare with the tremendous vitality and aesthetic quality of the pre-Columbian artists. Though much of the contemporary clay work is amusing, and often has touches of real charm, it is vastly inferior to such examples as are illustrated in Plates 25, 33 or 48. Present-day Totonac artists show no relationship to their Veracruz predecessors, who left behind such figurines as those in Plates 66 or 70. Today, most pottery is essentially utilitarian, and occasionally vessels are seen which have real beauty; perhaps the most characteristic examples of this range are the blackware vessels of Coyotepec (Plates 221).

In southern Mexico, including the Yucatán peninsula, the major Indian arts have largely disappeared; Mayan craftsmen came and went, leaving exciting hints of their genius in the archaeological ruins and cemeteries. Little of this greatness is to be found among the surviving Mayan tribes —pottery and textiles are still produced, but not in the quantity or quality of former times. The strongest visual relationship may be seen in the Lacandón " god pots," still in use as bowls for burning copal incense; the faces modeled on these grotesque *incensarios* show a resemblance to the Mayapán pottery in Plate 94. The Mayan-speaking Tzeltal and Tzotzil have retained some facets of their earlier life, but little which can be regarded as aesthetically significant.

Threads of Mayan Life; the Highland Weavers. The most vibrant Mayan art expressions to be found today are in the interior highland villages of Guatemala. Here the major aesthetic accomplishment is weaving, and no other region in the Americas offers such a rich variety. Some of the textiles produced by Navajo Indians in the Southwestern United States and in the Andean highlands of South America are remarkable in design and skill, but these are essentially the result of a single weaving technique. What is particlarly impressive about the Quiché and Cakchiquel weavers is the tremendous range of forms and exuberant color employed in these arts. From simple garments with delicate trim to the most elaborately worked *huipil* with baroque design and blazing color combinations which rival the rainbow, the vital force of this art is evident (Plate 228). Spanish influence is undeniable in these textiles, but it is subjugated to what is clearly an Indian art form. The weaver uses aboriginal technology in a unique manner (Plate 229).

Equally astonishing is the vast quantity of textiles still produced. Yardage for women's skirts, material for blouses, headgear, and other needs are all turned out, literally by the mile. It is not unusual to see thousands of yards of freshly dyed yarn stretched along the roadside, drying in the sun; one length recently examined was measured off by the automobile speedometer at just over four miles. When textiles are being turned out in this quantity, the art is certainly far from expiring, whatever else may happen.

And these are fabrics of high quality. The market in Guatemala is a demanding combination of knowledgeable Indian and discriminating tourist customers; perhaps no other Indian art in Middle America has "arrived" to the degree that these textiles have. Sports costumes, skirtings, and many other forms have found wide acceptance in specialty shops throughout the world.

This demand for such large quantities has required the introduction of the horizontal, or treadle, loom which is used today for most of the yard goods. The aboriginal belt loom is reserved for producing narrower widths of material for belts, shawls, *huipil* manufacture, and similar items. Although native dyes were usual in earlier days, the custom today is to use native cottons and color them with commercial dyes. In the larger lengths, ready-dyed-and-spun commercial yarns are more commonly employed. As is inevitable, textile factories have been set up; and these must be, if the demand is to be met and the craft is to survive. Just so long as integrity and taste do not disappear, the result will be a strong progressive force in Indian art.

The other arts have not kept pace with the weaver; wood carving, by and large, is crude in comparison to what it must have been in ancient times. Stone carving is almost non-existent today, aside from knickknacks made for the souvenir trade; the latter are usually grotesque creations lacking any of the aesthetic strength and clean line of the ancient Maya. The once-great complex of mask carving continues, although in a somewhat attenuated form. Although examples of animal masks seem more overtly to reflect aboriginal use (Plate 224), the tremendous variety of human face designs with heavy beards is obviously derived from traditions introduced by European wood carvers. Plate 227 illustrates the imposition of these designs upon aboriginal forms; many are carved by *mestizos*—that is, persons with both Indian and White blood, who thus combine both traditions in their bodies as well as in their arts. Even

the ceremonies in which these masks are used manifest an often bizarre combination of Christian and pagan practice; the problem of unraveling the threads of this complex fabric would challenge even the most astute anthropological detective.

These carved masks have little outside demand; at least, not to the extent of that enjoyed by textiles, and therefore they have not been affected as greatly by other than local needs. They are still produced primarily for ceremonial use, and the one factor which has a bearing upon their external appearance has been the appearance of small family factories which produce masks for a wide range of Indian customers, often renting them out for a given ceremony; the same mask may thus be used in several villages (and the regalia as well).

Designs tend to become somewhat more standardized as they are employed over a wide area. Contrary to North American Indian practice, particularly in the Southwest, is the fact that although these masks are not made primarily for sale to outsiders, such disposal does not offend nor outrage the Indian in the slightest.

Although pottery in this region has undergone considerable change, it is still manufactured in quantity, and even the plain, undecorated utility objects are beautifully formed. The redware vessel in Plate 225 is a fine example of contemporary ceramics; it comes, a thousand years later, from the same area as did the specimens in Plates 109 and 119. It is much less elaborate, but it retains the strength and the simple grace of those masterpieces.

The quality that is remarkably apparent in this region is the sense of quiet dignity and self-containment which is so evident. It cannot be denied that European contact has made its effect upon the lives of these people, yet without obliterating the Indian qualities to the extent one finds in Mexico. In the latter region, by and large, Indian essence is present, but secondary to the European characteristics; in Guatemala, the reverse seems true.

Just a few miles away, the Nahuatl-speaking Pipil of El Salvador, distant cousins of the Aztecs, though not of Mayan ancestry, manifest interesting influences of the latter peoples in some of their arts. The monkey jar in Plate 232 is of a redware very similar in texture and color to that in Plate 225; but of even more interest is the tie-and-dye skirting material in Plate 230. The design and weaving techniques are identical to much of the *jaspe* yardage woven by highland Guatemala weavers; only the colors would cause the viewer to question the place of origin. It is not unlikely that this may be an introduced art from the adjoining area.

Outposts of Survival; South to the Isthmus. Other isolated cultural remnants include the Sumu and Miskito in neighboring Honduras and Nicaragua. These folk have been pushed into the background of these countries, and the introduction during the last century of Negro workers along the Gulf Coast has made the maintenance of any cultural identity extremely difficult. Perhaps the most interesting Indian carry-over is the masking complex used at the Miskito Feast of the Dead (Plate 234); these bark costumes are not unlike similar ceremonial dress farther to the south. Indeed, it is with this area that we come into an increasing indication of these southerly influences. In this meeting ground of north and south, it is evident that the cultural interchanges have not been a one-way street. In northern Middle America, there was a distinct infiltration into the southern United States, while in the central area, movements were in both directions. But as one travels farther to the south, the influences are seemingly more distinctly from South America into the isthmus, with only secondary extensions from Mexico southward.

As just one example of what this means, although the Nahuatl-speaking tribes extended at one time from the Aztec in Mexico south to the Nicarao in Nicaragua—and included a few small pockets in Panama—it does not imply that these all reflected the same art form. They blended with the indigenous peoples they encountered, and developed a new expression. This does, however, explain some of the many confusing features which so often face the student in examining these peripheral culture regions. And these new types or " phases " would be greatly affected by the relative strength of the host culture; evironment, natural resources, and extent of population all play a part.

The Jicaque, the Paya and the Lenca have little left of their aboriginal aesthetic work. Some fugitive traits are still being practiced, as the pottery in Plate 232 and the unique style of decorating gourd rattles (Plates 233); but in the main, little can be found today which represents the earlier arts of these people. None of the great ceramic traditions have survived, and the clay work in general has yielded to the tin gasoline can and the oil-drum containers.

In Costa Rica, the Boruca people, a division of the larger Talamancan group, are (along with the Cábecar, Bribri and the Térraba) residual folk from a once more populous representation. The statement that no Indians exist today in Costa Rica is patently incorrect; it is true, however, that their numbers are small, and their homeland is extremely isolated. The degree to which these units have been able to maintain themselves and their culture is represented by the textile arts (Plate 235) and the use of carved masks (Plate 236). This latter is in surprising strength, although little is known of the ceremonial aspects of the custom.

The Nicarao, Chorotega, and Güetar are no longer in evidence; while a few survivors may have blended in with other Indians, it is unlikely that any identifiable individuals exist; and none of these demonstrate the aesthetic proficiency of their forebears to the degree represented in Plates 148, 153, or 162. Indeed, one of the tragedies is the complete disappearance of some of these arts; in view of the tremendous amount of gold work which we know existed in prehistoric times, it is astonishing that no Indian tribes of the region carry on this art today. Even those fraudulent examples of " pre-Columbian gold " which are in such evidence in the shops today are made by non-Indian workmen!

To examine indigenous culture in any degree in southern Middle America today, the last outpost would be Panama. Here the Guaymí Indians in Coclé and Chriquí provinces have managed to retain a limited amount of their aboriginal culture in the more remote areas. Their arts reflect a considerable acculturation, to be sure; but the effects are largely in the introduction of new materials, as in the beaded collar in Plate 237; certainly the calabash decoration would appear not to have been influenced by outside forms (Plate 239). The bark costume (Plate 238) seemingly reflects more of the effects of contact with other Indian tribes than with Europeans—even though trousers made from bark cloth have been incorporated into the costume.

A more interesting blend of influence is found among the Cuna, living on the San Blas Islands off the mainland. These insular people have not only held their lands to themselves, but have managed to secure a degree of political recognition. And, although their life is slowly undergoing change, they have been able to hold this abrasive force stubbornly at arm's length, yielding ever so slowly. Objects will reflect Indian usage, yet include European motifs; for example, it is not unusual to see a *mola*, basically Indian in design, with "Pepsi-Cola" emblazoned across the breast —or a prehistoric pottery design worked into the blouse will be broken by a ship sailing along under full steam, in many colors of cotton cloth.

The religious arts survive in considerable strength; the carved wooden shaman's figurines are still important, even though some are sold to tourists visiting the islands (Plate 241), and others often portray European characters (Plate 245). The graceful plumed headdresses retain their cultural importance, and are as highly prized as ever (Plate 243).

Yet the gold these Indians wear as ornamentation, particularly the ubiquitous nose ring formerly worn by almost all Cuna women, are fashioned in Panama City, many by Chinese goldsmiths. No Indian goldsmiths are active at the present time, but this custom of using gold nose rings, breast plaques, and earrings clearly demonstrates the manner in which ancient gold jewelry was worn and treasured by the pre-Conquest Indians.

In Darién, the isthmian area adjoining northern South America, one would rightly expect to find the most aboriginal groups—and this is the case. The Chocó Indians, living in the jungle fastness of Panama which has still balked the efforts of the Pan-American Highway construction engineers, have had but little contact with the non-Indian world. None of these people are entirely ignorant of the Withie man, of course; but intrusions are relatively irregular and of short duration. Their arts probably reflect about as "pure" an Indian form as one can expect to encounter in the area encompassed by this volume. The basketry has been affected not at all (Plate 242), even though tin cans have begun to replace some of the larger storage containers. The ceremonial wood carvings still used by Chocó shamans are less Europeanized than the same objects found among the Cuna—yet again, occasionally a European will be depicted in such carvings (Plate 246); curing boards are still much the same as they were in earlier years (Plate 247), and the ingeniously woven dance leader's crown is probably but little different from those worn centuries ago (Plate 248).

Threadbare Remnants; the Islands of the Caribbean. It is safe to say that, of all the areas considered in this book, none have lost their aboriginal characteristics so completely as have the people of the West Indies. This is largely due to a deliberate exploitation to the point of annihilation; once the Spaniard arrived, they set the Indians to work mining the gold which was then somewhat common on several of the larger islands. Proving intractable as slaves, the Indians were killed off, removed to other areas, or died from disease. Within twenty-five years after the arrival of Columbus, the population had so declined that the Spaniards had to import slaves from Africa to work the gold mines; by 1700, the population of the West Indies was 80 percent Negroid.

Further decline in Indian population, natural increase of the Negro immigrants, and subsequent changes in insular make-up account for the present complexion of the islands. In seeking Indian cultural remnants in the West Indies today the only possible fragment is represented by a tiny handful—about 250 at most—living in the Baracoa area of Cuba. None of these are full-blooded, nor have they retained any degree of Indian cultural expression, other than a small amount of basketry. The great stone-carving arts of their ancestors, as illustrated in Plates 198, 200, or 204 are all completely gone—nor do they produce any of the wood carving or pottery once prevalent in the islands.

New Art Forms; Invention and Innovations. In recent years, a wave of interest in the antiquity of Middle America and its arts has given rise to various aesthetic innovations, some of which have been healthy, and more which have been injurious. The intelligent application of old forms, well designed for contemporary use, has not been as prevalent as might be desired. There is a place for such artistic modernization and adaptation, but all too often the goal is the production of souvenirs and knickknacks without consideration for the longer-term avenue by which even greater results can be achieved, in terms both of human qualities and financial rewards.

The successes of such men as Daniel Rubín de la Borbolla and William Spratling in reviving Mexican arts is exemplary of the manner in which life can be put back into what may have seemed lost arts; the need is for more people of their technical and aesthetic stature to work among the undeveloped pools of ability which are to be found on every hand in Middle America. As they have demonstrated so ably, the enterprising genius who sets out to salvage the life of a people must know when to keep hands off—as well as when to step in with firm guidance.

In an entirely different field of artistic innovation is the increasing amount of fraudulent work being produced.

Of the stone carving offered for sale today in Mexico, and represented as being "pre-Columbian," it is safe to say that less than half can claim an ancestry of more than fifty years. The proportion of fraudulent ceramic work, most particularly of the Veracruz, Jalisco, Colima or Nayarit styles, is increasingly evident; other arts have been proportionately affected. In the south, most notably Costa Rica and Panama, much of the gold work offered as "genuine pre-Columbian art" is produced by melting down archaeological gold and recasting it in modern molds.

The detection of such fraudulent material is extremely difficult; although some can be readily identified, many are so skillfully worked as to defy the most expert eye. Ancestry means little, for this is not just a recent practice—many of the "old" fakes in collections can be traced well back into the early nineteenth century.

The extent of Middle American interest in maintenance of native arts varies considerably. In most countries it must be admitted that concern for the survival of native elements in the culture is very slight; lip service is occasionally given such efforts, but rarely does it go beyond this. In a few countries, most notably in Mexico and Guatemala, governmental departments have been established to work with the native Indian population; these include sub-departments dedicated to the perpetuation of the arts. A few folk art museums have been established, most of which include Indian art materials in their collections.

The conserving forces of public interest can exert a healthy effect upon this situation, provided a wise balance is maintained. If preoccupation with antiquity continues in single-minded fashion to ignore post-Columbian art expressions, the disappearance of the latter can only be hastened—for just as it prevents the development of a respect for Indian art among the non-Indians, it takes from the living Indian artist any reason for pride in his own culture. And with the introduction of new values, change in functions, and removal of the native market, many of the purposes for continuation are lost. Most tragic of all is the attitude that, somehow, "being different is inferior."

This amalgamation of the old and the new is not in itself necessarily bad, however loudly some may bewail it. If the amalgamation is wisely accomplished, improvement can result. If changes are simply an indiscriminate adoption of the new, both good and bad, the results will be disastrous. But if the best features of both worlds are allowed to meld gracefully, a vital force can emerge which will make a significant contribution to the new society. This can only come from the development of an informed, appreciative audience.... the major purpose of this volume.

PLATES AND COMMENTARIES

1 *MODELED CLAY FIGURINE*

These stylized human forms, often bifurcated, are found in a small area centering around Kino Bay, the present-day home of the Seri Indians; they are thought to have been made by their ancestors. Usually found buried a few inches below the surface, as many as ten have been discovered arranged together in a circle. Nothing is known of their purpose; burned material found with them suggests a funerary use. The indented decoration on the torso may indicate body tattooing, a common Seri practice today.

KINO VIEJO; Sonora, Mexico   Proto-historic
Museum of the American Indian: 22/5614   H: 5 ½ in.

2 *"FEATHERED SERPENT" BOWL*

The use of this design extends from the southwestern United States deep into Mesoamerica, and may represent a similar distribution of ceremonial customs linked to the Quetzalcóatl legend. The serpent's body continues on around the vessel; a more angular design than typically found farther south, it is characteristic of the classic work of the Casas Grandes potters.

CASAS GRANDES; Chihuahua, Mexico   1000-1500
Museum of the American Indian: 11/9739   H: 11 ½ in.

3 *POLYCHROME EFFIGY VESSEL*

The duck's head emerges smoothly from the rotund form of the body in this crisply painted bowl; the modeled wings and tail balance this neatly. These vessels often show little indication of wear, suggesting that their function was primarily for funerary offering —a trait common to all of Middle America and parts of North America.

CASAS GRANDES; Chihuahua, Mexico   1000-1500
Museum of the American Indian: 11/9782   H: 6 ½ x 11 in.

4 *STANDING FEMALE FIGURE*

Usually the soils of Mexico remove the painted surfaces of painted clay objects; the amount which has survived on this specimen is remarkable. Her textile headband and skirt are identical with contemporary Indian dress, and the custom of tattooing the body has only recently disappeared. She is carrying a small pottery *olla*. See Plate 5.

IXTLÁN DEL RÍO; Nayarit, Mexico   300-1250

Museum of the American Indian: 23/2275   H: 14 ½ in.

5 PAINTED MALE FIGURE

A companion piece to Plate 4, this male effigy was
found in the same burial; like it, there is a major
amount of original paint remaining. This man is
shown holding a mace, or a fan; his costume consists
of textiles and a peculiar conical hat. The shell
penis-cover is typical of the area. The grotesque art
of the ancient Tarascan potters is nowhere more clearly
demonstrated than in this pair. See Plate 4.

IXTLÁN DEL RÍO; Nayarit, Mexico   300-1250
Museum of the American Indian: 23/2276   H: 20 ½ in.

6 TWO-HEADED ANIMAL EFFIGY

It is difficult to determine what the maker had in mind with this effigy—he certainly was not working from a live model! This dual-headed form is similar to other effigies, both animal and human, found in Mexico. In spite of the unusual form, the grace and composition of this specimen is extremely effective.

Jamulco; Nayarit, Mexico   300-1250

Museum of the American Indian: 22/5715   H: 10 x 14 in.

7 PAINTED POTTERY BOWL

If one can judge by collections available today, it would seem that anthropomorphic figures were more commonly made than simple vessels in ancient times. This effectively decorated example is evidence that the potters did not restrict themselves to any single style of work. Gift of John S. Williams.

Ixtlán del Río; Nayarit, Mexico   300-1250

Museum of the American Indian: 22/5083   D: 8 ½ in.

8 FIGURE OF A BALL-PLAYER

Typical of western Mexican ceramic sculpture, this male figure wears the costume common to ball-players. In his left hand he holds the type of solid rubber ball which was used in the ancient game. Photograph by Ferdinand Anton.

OCOTLÁN; Jalisco, Mexico   300-900
National Museum of Anthropology, Mexico   H: 11 in.

9 GROUP OF STONE MACE-HEADS

These finely worked implements are found in the region around Jalisco and Michoacán, and are not unlike some ax heads from Guerrero. They were presumably fastened to wooden shafts, although their precise function is not clearly understood. The skill in fashioning them shows a long development in stone cutting skills.

JALISCO, Mexico   500-1000
Museum of the American Indian: Longest: 4 in.
    15/5654, 20/22, 20/23, 6/6389

10 *MODELED CLAY MADONNA*

This magnificent example of the potter's art is notable
not only for its size, and the amount of paint remaining
on the figure, but equally for the plastic quality of
the sculpturing. It is one of many which present
the theme of a woman nursing her baby.

MAGDALENA; Jalisco, Mexico   300-900
Museum of the American Indian: 22/5713   H: 18 in.

11 *SEATED FEMALE FIGURE*

Modeled in red clay, with buffware face, this delicately
worked effigy is painted in the style customary for the
region, although much of the original decoration is
now lost. The hair is indicated by carefully incised
lines; the holes in the ears duplicate those pierced
in life for insertion of decorative earrings.

LOS ORTICES; Colima, Mexico   300-950
Museum of the American Indian: 16/3639   H: 9 ½ in.

12 *MUSICIAN IN COSTUME*

The ancient Mexican tendency to depict everday life in clay figurines is shown in this standing musician; such sculptures are helpful in unraveling prehistoric cultural activities. He wears a pointed cap, and may have once had copper earrings in his ears. On his back is an elaborate fan-shaped feather ornament used in ancient ceremonies. In his right hand he holds a short stick with which he rhythmically strokes the long notched musical rasp. Gift of John S. Williams.

COLIMA; Colima, Mexico   300-1250
Museum of the American Indian: 22/8838   H: 17 in.

13 "EL PENSADOR" EFFIGY

The viewer is irresistibly drawn to a comparison of this meditating figurine with the classic bronze by Rodin, even at the risk of reading too much into the sculpture. The flowing lines of the body and the plastic modeling of the head make this a masterpiece of western Mexican pottery art. Gift of John S. Williams.

BUENA VISTA; Colima, Mexico   300-1250
Museum of the American Indian: 22/5100   H: 8 ½ in.

14 POLISHED REDWARE BOWL

The pottery from this small area is remarkable for its unique quality; the style is found nowhere else in the Americas. The fluted body of this globular vessel is supported by three legs, each of which is modeled in the form of a bird with folded wings.

COLIMA; Colima, Mexico   300-1250
Museum of the American Indian: 23/1635   10 ¼ x 14 ½ in.

15 *EFFIGY OF A WRESTLER*

The characteristic dwarfed arms, so frequently used in western Mexican clay sculpture, present a strange contrast to the powerful torso and legs of this figurine. Withal, the body is strongly balanced.

CoLIMA; Colima, Mexico   300-1250
Museum of the American Indian: 23/208   H: 10 in.

16 *POLYCHROME GLOBULAR BOWL*

The stylized treatment of the face, with the fret-outlined eyes and modeled nose and mouth, is characteristic of the redware pottery from this famous site. These sleek, highly polished rotund vessels are representative of some of the finest central Mexican ceramics.

CHUPÍCUARO; Guanajuato, Mexico   300 B.C.-300 A.D.
Museum of the American Indian: 23/1076   4½ x 9 in.

17 *PAINTED FEMALE FIGURINE*

Made in a bewildering variety of forms, these tiny clay figurines show the great detail and fine modeling applied to early figurines from the western coastal region of Mexico. The purpose of these numerous human figures is unknown.

CHUPÍCUARO; Guanajuato, Mexico   300 B.C.-300 A.D.
Museum of the American Indian: 21/7294   H: 4 in.

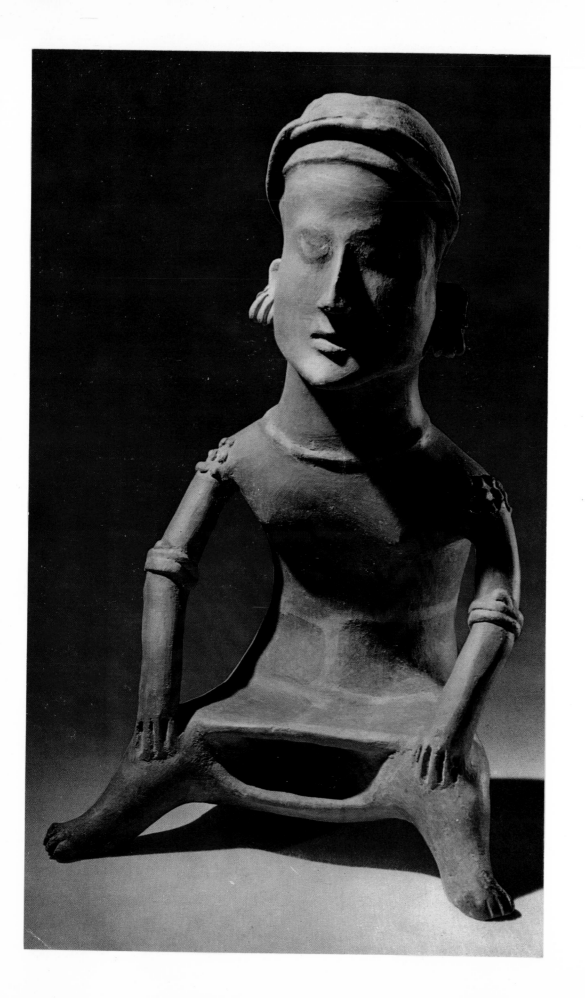

18 *FIGURE OF A SEATED WOMAN*

Another type of clay modeling is shown in this effigy of a woman who is seated on a low bench, which does not show in the illustration. Much of the original paint has been lost, although the clay work is intact. Her copper earrings show plainly.

MICHOACÁN, Mexico   300-950
Museum of the American Indian: 22/1359   H: 18 ½ in.

19 *STIRRUP-HANDLED VESSEL*

A beautifully modeled vessel with an elongated pouring spout and molded handle. The latter is an extension of a pottery form which has a wide distribution throughout the Western Hemisphere. Photograph by Ferdinand Anton.

TZINTZUNTZÁN; Michoacán, Mexico   1250-1500
National Museum of Anthropology, Mexico   7 ¹/₈ x 8 ³/₄ in.

20 *CLAY INCENSARIO COVERS*

While the actual use of these *tapaderas* is not known, it is believed they were covers for incense burners. Their forms vary, and it is probable that they may not have covered a brazier, but may simply have been placed over a burning bit of copal placed in a depression in the ground.

CAPIRAL; Michoacán, Mexico   500-1000
Museum of the American Indian: 23/114, 22/7134   H: 7 ½ in.

21 *CLASSIC STONE FIGURINE*

Representative of the most typical Teotihuacán style, this carved stone figurine may at one time have been inlaid with shell; the small circular depressions suggest such usage. The incised lines represent a textile garment. These effigies, usually in a black or green stone, are found in various sizes distributed over a large area of central Mexico.

TEOTIHUACÁN; Mexico, Mexico   250-600
Museum of the American Indian: 10/7462   H: 12 in.

22 *STONE OCELOT RECEPTACLE*

This famous *Ocelocuauhxicalli* is carved of basalt in the form of an ocelot, and has a cavity in the back in which sacrificial offerings were placed. It has a feline quality effective for its powerful composition combined with a flowing, graceful line. Photograph by Ferdinand Anton.

VALLEY OF MEXICO; Mexico   1500-1521
National Museum of Anthropology, Mexico   L: 7 ft. 4 in.

23 *STATUTE OF XIPE TOTEC*

Set up as standard bearers outside Aztec temples, these stylized statues of volcanic stone represent *Xipe Totec*, The Flayed God, and show a priest dressed in the skin of a victim. This specimen is remarkable not only for its aesthetic quality, but also for the carved cartouche on the back indicating the date *1 Acatl* (1507 A.D.), the year in which the New Fire was kindled in the 52-year cyclical calendar. Presumably this indicates the date of erection of this statue. Part of the original paint is still visible.

TEPEPÁN; Mexico, Mexico   1507 A.D.
Museum of the American Indian: 16/3621   H: 30 ½ in.

24 CACAO-POD FIGURE

This exquisite little figure of a man carrying a cacao pod exemplifies the quiet beauty of much of Aztec stone art. It retains a great deal of the original red paint with which it was once covered. Photograph by Ferdinand Anton.

AMATLÁN; Veracruz, Mexico   1000-1500
Brooklyn Museum of Art   H: 14 in.

25 FIRE GOD EFFIGY

This is one of the finest examples of thin orange ware known from Mexico. The modeling is extremely sensitive, and the proportions of the vessel make it a masterpiece of ceramic artistry. The figure is that of *Huehuetéotl*, a major deity in the Teotihuacán pantheon. Gift of Mrs. Thea Heye.

TOLUCA; Mexico, Mexico   250-650
Museum of the American Indian: 16/6067   H: 12 ½ in.

26 CARVED OLMEC FIGURINE

A beautifully worked example of the Olmec artist's skill in carving, this black stone figurine is typical of the early horizon of Mexican culture. It is one of the prizes in the collection gathered by the late Miguel Covarrubias. Photograph courtesy of the Instituto Nacional de Antropología e Historia.

MEXICO; Mexico   800 B.C.-100 A.D.
National Museum of Anthropology, Mexico   H: 6 in.

28 MINIATURE FIGURINES

Tiny clay figurines are found throughout the Teotihuacán area in modest numbers. Made in several distinct styles, and over a long period of time, their actual use is not known.

TEOTIHUACÁN; Mexico, Mexico   200 B.C.-250 A.D.
Museum of the American Indian: H: 2 ½, 3 ¾ in.
    23/897, 22/1370

27 PAINTED CLAY MASKETTE

This diminutive maskette is mold-made in thin-walled clay. The painted decoration, of black and red lines on a white base, may still be seen clearly. It is of the classic Teotihuacán type, and should be compared with similar forms in Plates 21 and 42.

TEOTIHUACÁN; Mexico, Mexico   250-600
Museum of the American Indian: 22/9144   3 ½ x 4 ½ in.

29 *COVER FOR AN INCENSE BURNER*

Elaborate incensers, made up of dozens of mold-made clay parts, were common in Middle America. Extremely fragile, they are usually found in fragments, and must be painstakingly put back together. Unfortunately, this restoration is often done with more imagination than accuracy, and the original appearance is sometimes lost in the process. The present example is an effort to attain as reasonably true a restoration of the original as practicable. A bowl-shaped brazier completes these vessels. Gift of The Viking Fund.

Azcapotzalco; Mexico, Mexico   500-750
Museum of the American Indian: 21/1243   H: 24 in.

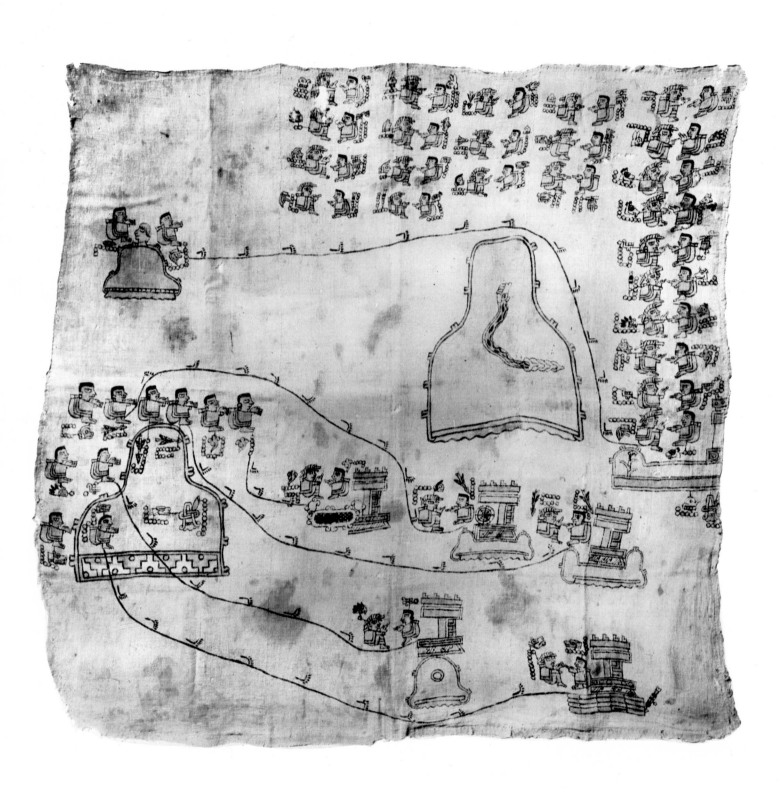

30 PAINTED LIENZO

The Mexican scribes used native cotton sheeting, upon which they painted designs and symbols in a form of hieroglyphic writing. It was the nearest to a written language achieved by the people of central Mexico, and those *lienzos* which have survived are invaluable as a key to an understanding of some aspects of their life. This example narrates the account of a journey made by several nobles; the name of each person is attached to his body by a line. The towns visited are indicated by appropriate *cartouche* sketches. See also Plate 59. Photograph courtesy of the University Museum.

MIXTEC; Oaxaca, Mexico   *ca.* 1500
University Museum: 42-7-1   42 ½ x 50 in.

31 CENTRAL MEXICAN POTTERY

This trio presents a variety of pottery forms from later periods common to the central plateau of Mexico just prior to the coming of the Spaniards. These wares are in several colors, usually a red polished base with black linear designs, often with incised decorations added. The surfaces are usually polished.

OZUMBA and TEOTIHUACÁN; Mexico, Mexico   250-1500
Museum of the American Indian: Tallest: 9 in.
   12/1503, 23/1819, 16/3396

32 *POTTERY MASK*

These are among the oldest clay masks yet found in the Mesoamerican region. They are made in a wide range of sizes, and many are so small as to preclude any possibility of their having been worn, thus suggesting some symbolic usage yet dimly understood.

TLATILCO; Mexico, Mexico   1000 B.C.-250 A.D.
Museum of the American Indian: 22/4684   H: 6 1/4 in.

33 *CLAY FIGURINE GROUP*

The amazingly wide variety of modeled clay figurines produced in ancient central Mexico is amply demonstrated by this assemblage, which shows both style and size of the " pretty ladies." Many poses and combinations are also known from this cultural complex, all of which relate to the Tlatilco sequence.

MEXICO; Mexico   1000 B.C.-250 A.D.
Museum of the American Indian   Tallest: 5 1/2 in.

34 POTTERY VESSELS

The potters of Tlatilco were not only skilled figurine modelers, but also produced many varieties of fine ware, three examples of which are illustrated. The shapes are of particular interest, and the stirrup-spouted vessel is similar to others found farther south.

TLATILCO; Mexico, Mexico   1000 B.C.-250 A.D.
Museum of the American Indian: Tallest: 10 in.
  22/9286, 23/2267, 22/5674

35 QUETZALCÓATL INCENSER

This *incensario* cover is a remarkable specimen. *Quetzalcóatl* is seated on a throne, holding his feathered serpent symbol. The hand-modeled clay feathering and detail testifies to the admirable patience of the potter and gives an over-all effect of baroque fussiness. The mold-made paneling and "wings" retain most of their original blue paint; traces of other colors suggest the brilliant original appearance of the object. Gift of the Marion Eppley Memorial Fund.

TEOTIHUACÁN; Mexico, Mexico   500-650
Museum of the American Indian: 23/899   10 ¼ x 11 ½ in.

36 SCULPTURED FRIEZE DETAIL

The original facing has been reapplied to the restored base of this structure to show its construction and appearance. Examination of the design reveals Mayan influence, although this site is quite distant from the Mayan heartland. Photograph by Ferdinand Anton.

XOCHICALCO; Morelos, Mexico   500 B.C.-500 A.D.

37 FIGURINE TRIO

These three clay figurines are representative of the variety found in this one small area in central Mexico. Comparison with Plate 32 shows similarities in facial structure, indicating a not-too-distant relationship.

GUALUPITA; Morelos, Mexico   500 B.C.-250 A.D.
Museum of the American Indian: Tallest: 13 in.
21/8816, 22/1349, 22/1351

38 *COVERED EFFIGY JAR*

Modeled from a light brown clay, this beautifully worked vessel was possibly used as a container for someone's valued jewelry or other personal effects. Said to have been excavated at Teotihuacán, it has a remarkable resemblance to some of the covered jars of this type found at Tikal and Kaminaljuyu (see Plate 105). Photograph courtesy of the American Museum of Natural History.

TEOTIHUACÁN; Mexico, Mexico   250-750
American Museum of Natural History: T109/186   H: 11 ½ in.

39 *CELTIFORM FIGURINES*

Each of these is basically derived from the form of the utilitarian stone celt. Apparently, over a long period of time, the technique of depicting the human form underwent considerable change in the Mezcala Valley. This trio clearly demonstrates how the sculptor reduced the elements of the body to its simplest form.

MEZCALA VALLEY; Guerrero, Mexico   500 B.C.-250 A.D.
Museum of the American Indian: Tallest: 7 in.
   21/8291, 15/5667, 18/9300

40 *CARVED OLMEC MASK*

The region southwest of Mexico City is renowned for the great number and variety of carved stone masks found there; many are of exceptional aesthetic quality, and seem to date from an early period. The present example manifests strong Olmec influences. See also Plate 61 and 78.

AYUTLA; Guerrero, Mexico   1000 B.C.-250 A.D.
Museum of the American Indian: 15/5783   H: 4 in.

41 *STONE FIRE GOD*

This brooding figurine is a powerful example of the art of sculptors in south-central Mexico. It represents *Huehuetéotl,* the Fire God also depicted in Plate 25, but in much smaller compass. Gift of James B. Ford.

SAN JERÓNIMO; Guerrero, Mexico   IA.D.-500
Museum of the American Indian: 9/3162   H: 6 in.

42 CLASSIC GREENSTONE MASK

The actual use of these is not clearly understood, although we do know that some were placed on statues, figurines, and on the bodies of the deceased. Some may also have served as decorations. The drilled holes are for the insertion of decorative accessories, such as feathers or flowers. This, of the classic Teotihuacán style, may be compared with Plates 21 and 27.

TEOTIHUACÁN; Mexico, Mexico   250-600
Museum of the American Indian: 20/3927   5 x 5 in.

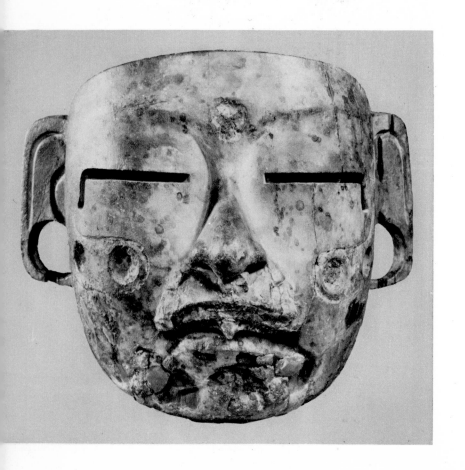

43 INLAID WOODEN MASK

At one time this magnificent mask was inlaid with jade, remnants of which may still be seen; it is probable that the ears also held jade ear plugs. Discovered in a cave in Guerrero, it is believed to be the only wooden object presently known to have survived from the Olmec period. Photograph courtesy of the American Museum of Natural History.

CAÑÓN DE LA MESA; Guerrero, Mexico   1000 B.C.-500 A.D.
American Museum of Natural History: 30.2/9373   7 x 8 in.

44 *POLYCHROME VASE*

These elaborately painted vessels tremendously impressed the Spaniards, who regarded them as being far superior to the ceramics then produced in Spain. The designs vary in symbolic content; the example illustrated shows shields, and the ubiquitous skull. These are combined in an over-all composition of attractive contrast. Collected in 1875 by Leo Stein. Gift of Mrs. Thea Heye.

CHOLULA; Puebla, Mexico   1350-1520
Museum of the American Indian: 16/3394   H: 10 in.

45 *MODELED CLAY INCENSARIO*

Of the type known as a *xantil,* this brilliantly painted modeled effigy vessel represents the God of Music and the Dance, *Macuilxochitl.* The hands are not missing; the peculiar arm sockets are normal for this type of object.

PUEBLA-VERACRUZ border; Mexico   1000-1500
Museum of the American Indian: 22/1603   H: 18 ½ in.

46 TURQUOISE MOSAIC SHIELD AND DETAIL

Thousands of tiny bits of turquoise were carefully cut and polished to form the delicate designs on this wooden *chimalli*. These shields were used for ceremonial purposes. Only the feathering which once rimmed the shield has been lost. The town sign is that of ancient Culhuacán. This is regarded as perhaps the finest single example of Mixtec mosaic art in turquoise; it was collected from a remote cave in Puebla sometime before 1900 by C. A. Purpus. Gift of James B. Ford.

ACATLÁN; Puebla, Mexico   1250-1500

Museum of the American Indian: 10/8708   D: 12 ½ in.

47 *WHEELED TOYS*

One can only repeat the cliché that the Amerindian knew of the wheel, but only as a toy; these two examples from widely separated areas validate that saying. The painted redware "dragon," actually a dog, originally had solid wooden axles; the buffware *caimán* probably used four individual axles; these have been restored in modern times. Gift of Dr. and Mrs. Frederick J. Dockstader.

HUAMANTLA; Tlaxcala, Mexico
IGNACIO DE LA LLAVE; Veracruz, Mexico   800-1250
Museum of the American Indian: 23/2171, 22/5562   L: 10 in.

48 *WHISTLING BOWL*

The god *Quetzalcóatl*, one of the major deities of Middle America, is depicted here with his begging bowl and feather fan; his headdress reflects the Feathered Serpent role, a symbol of his identity. The characteristic eye decoration and mouth ornament are indicated by paint. Although this vessel is of Mixtec origin, it is linked to a technique which extends from Mexico to Peru: when liquid is poured from the bowl, the expulsion of air produces a low, whistling sound.

PUEBLA; Puebla, Mexico   1250-1500
Museum of the American Indian: 23/848   H: 6 in.

49 *PANORAMA OF MONTE ALBÁN*

One of the most spectacular ruins of prehistoric Mexico is the site at Monte Albán. Perhaps nowhere else can the viewer get as clear an understanding of the over-all layout and architectural arrangement of space as in this classic capital. Photograph by Ferdinand Anton.

MONTE ALBÁN; Oaxaca, Mexico   500 B.C.-1500 A.D.

50 *PAINTED TRIPOD BOWL*

These two views show the outside form and interior decoration of a classic Mixtec polychrome vessel. The whole composition is symbolic of the ever-present Feathered Serpent. Photography by Ferdinand Anton.

MITLA; Oaxaca, Mexico   1000-1500
Museo Regional Frissell, Mexico   H: 6 1/8 in.

51 *FUNERARY URN*

Modeled and mold-made clay vessels of this design were made in large numbers by the Zapotec people for deposition in tombs as burial offerings. They were used both as containers for valuable objects and as *incensarios*. The designs are many; most show deities, identified by the *adornos* or attributes, some are animals, while a few may represent the deceased personage.

MONTE ALBÁN; Oaxaca, Mexico   250-500
Museum of the American Indian: 16/3623   H: 24 in.

52 *CARVED STONE PLAQUE*

These are the most characteristic types of carving found in the Mixtec region. They are found of serpentine, jadeite, nephrite and related minerals, and usually called "jade." The Mixtec technique of carving by various-sized drills is clearly shown in the illustration; far more time-consuming techniques were required to produce the carved stones in Plates 58 and 139.

MITLÁ; Oaxaca, Mexico   1000-1500
Museum of the American Indian: 1/2548   L: 5⁷/₈ in.

53 *STANDING CLAY SCULPTURE*

The half-shaven hair treatment is occasionally seen on other Zapotec sculptures. Around the neck of this figure is a collar, presumably representing human upper jaws, while from the throat is suspended a decapitated human trophy head. In the right hand is a vessel shaped like a panther's paw, common in Zapotec ceramics. Around the waist is a belt made of shells. This remarkable figure was taken to France in 1845 by Monsieur Martin, the French consular agent at Oaxaca, who had collected it near Mitla some years before.

MITLÁ; Oaxaca, Mexico   *ca.* 1000?
Museum of the American Indian: 19/5806   H: 29 in.

54 *GOLD LABRET*

This superb example of the art of the Mixtec gold-smith was designed to be worn in the lower lip of an important personage. The forked tongue is so constructed as to swing freely; the cylindrical plug holds the labret securely in place. This hollow object weighs 51 grams, presenting a formidable weight to suspend from one's lower lip! Photograph courtesy of the American Museum of Natural History.

TLACOLULA; Oaxaca, Mexico   1200-1500
American Museum of Natural History: T66/1   2 ½ x 2 ⁵/₈ in.

55 *GOLD FINGER RINGS*

The skill of the Mixtec craftsman is amply demonstrated by this selection of gold jewelry. Made in a filigree pattern by the lost-wax process, these portray a human head, and two birds' heads (presumably eagles). The attachment of two tiny bells and a small forehead ornament only increases our admiration for the patient artist who created these treasures. Gift of Mrs. Thea Heye.

MONTE ALBÁN; Oaxaca, Mexico   1250-1500
Museum of the American Indian: H: 1 ³/₈ D: ⁷/₈ in.
16/3417, 16/3447, 20/6218

56 GOLD NECKLACE

This necklace of cast gold demonstrates the technical and aesthetic skill of the Mixtec goldsmith. It is composed of forty turtle-shell segments; from each is suspended pear-shaped pendants similar to gold bells common to the region. Gift of Mrs. Thea Heye.

SOLA DE VEGA; Oaxaca, Mexico   1250-1500
Museum of the American Indian: 16/3451   L: 14 in.

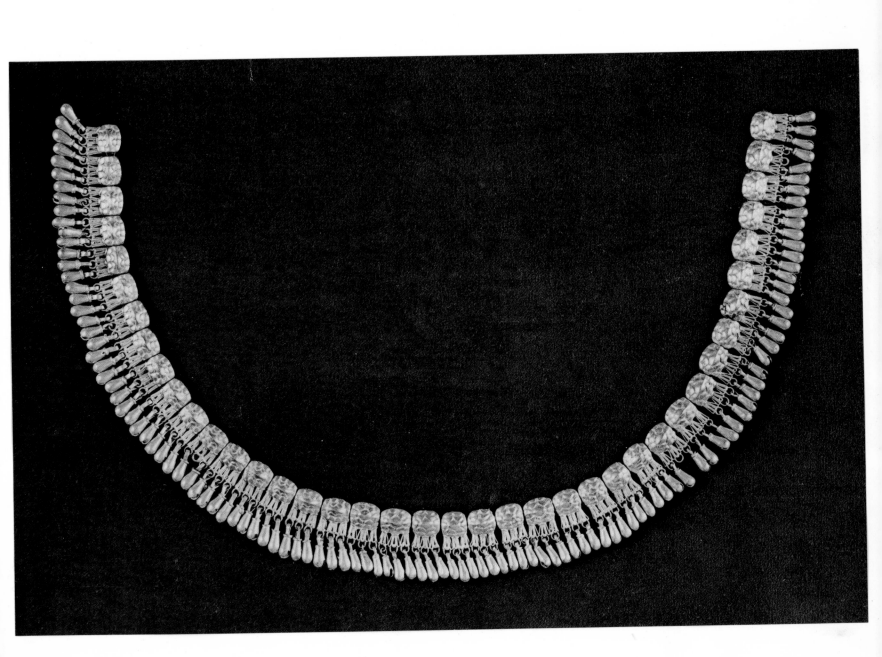

57 STONE MOSAIC FAÇADE

These intricate designs are not carved, as first glance would suggest, but are composed of thousands of pre-cut stones carefully fitted into a variety of mosaic patterns. Originally, the designs were emphasized by the addition of color, but most of this paint is now lost. Still in use at the time of the Conquest, this is one of several structures built by Mixtec architects who continued an earlier Zapotec tradition at this ceremonial center. Photograph by Ferdinand Anton.

MITLA; Oaxaca, Mexico   900-1500

58 CARVED JADE PLAQUE

This portrait of a Mayan dignitary shows him seated in the characteristic cross-legged pose so frequent in the art of this region. He wears an elaborately feathered headdress; the deep vertical line results from the technique employed to cut it away from a larger piece. This ornament was presumably worn suspended on the breast.

MONTE ALBÁN; Oaxaca, Mexico   500-900
Museum of the American Indian: 2/6671   2 ¼ x 3 ¼ in.

59 *THE DRESDEN CODEX*

Two pages from the oldest of the three surviving Mayan codices, showing the style of writing used by these early scribes. Although not fully deciphered, it is possible to transliterate enough of the document to know that it was an astronomical record. The similarity of these illuminated manuscripts to those of ancient Egypt, Persia, and medieval Europe is tragic evidence of what has been lost over the centuries in Middle America. The dating is uncertain; this codex was probably made sometime in the ninth or tenth century. Photography by Ferdinand Anton.

Staatliche Kunstsammlungen Dresden, Germany   3 ½ x 10 ½ in.

60 *CARVED STONE HACHA*

The smoothly fashioned features of this powerful stone head are balanced magnificently by the tenon, described in the text. This type of tenon should be compared with that commonly found farther south, as in Plate 108.

VERACRUZ; Veracruz, Mexico   750-1000
Museum of the American Indian: 16/3474   H: 11 ½ in.

61 GRANITE AX HEAD

These large anthropomorphic stone carvings are typical of the Olmec period in Mexico. Extremely rare, they are effective presentations of the so-called "baby face" design prevalent in the art of that culture. Their use is unknown; they are usually termed "votive axes" on the assumption that they had only a ceremonial function. Collected by Leo Stein sometime before 1880 "along the coast of Vera Cruz." Gift of Mrs. Thea Heye.

VERACRUZ, Mexico   1000 B.C.-250 A.D.
Museum of the American Indian: 16/3400   H: 11 ½ in.

62 PAINTED TRIPOD PLATE

The strong design styles on this pottery vessel are characteristic of a small burial site off the coast of Veracruz. The symbolism represents a dog sacrifice; the vessel has a pedestal support similar to that shown in Plate 186 from Panama.

ISLA DE SACRIFICIOS; Veracruz, Mexico   600-900
Museum of the American Indian: 23/653   D: 8 ⅛ in.

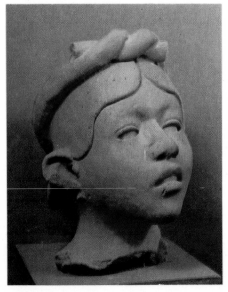

63 *HEAD OF A YOUNG GIRL*

This delicately modeled head is a fragment from a larger vessel. She is wearing a textile headdress, similar to the style still worn throughout Mexico and Guatemala. Photograph by Ferdinand Anton.

VERACRUZ, Mexico   500-750
Regional Museum of Jalapa, Veracruz   H: 3 ½ in.

64 *"LAUGHING FACE" EFFIGIES*

These happy clay creations are found by the hundreds in southern Veracruz. Formerly only the heads were known, but complete figures are now known, which reveal a wide assortment of types. These three examples present a range of type varieties; the cause for the fixed, stylized smile is as baffling as that of *La Gioconda*. Gifts of George Juergens and H. J. Browne.

LAS REMOJADAS; Veracruz, Mexico   250-900
Museum of the American Indian: Figure: 11 in.
    6/5439, 22/5855, 22/2312

65 *CARVED HEMATITE MIRROR*

The reverse side of this object has been polished smooth to provide a reflecting surface. The side illustrated portrays a young man wearing an elaborate headdress and a complex belt—or perhaps a yoke? —with a pendant sash. Gift of John S. Williams.

EL TAJÍN; Veracruz, Mexico   750-1000
Museum of the American Indian: 22/6252   D: 3 ³/₈ in.

66   *FIRE GOD PRIEST*

This clay figurine of an elaborately costumed personage may represent a Totonac version of a priest of *Xiuhtecuhtli,* the Fire God. He wears a maskette of the Fire God on his forehead, decorated with feathers. Suspended from a necklace is a large disk symbolic of his mirror, or shield. Around his waist is a ceremonial skirt. The two prominent teeth are also symbolic features of this god, who was known as *Huehuetéotl* in later Aztec times; his cult spread throughout Mesoamerica, as is seen by such examples as shown in Plates 25, 41, 85.

LAS REMOJADAS; Veracruz, Mexico   300-900
Museum of the American Indian: 22/6248   H: 16 ½ in.

67   *CARVED ONYX VASE*

Presumably made for sacrificial offerings, these are carved from *tecali,* a form of onyx often miscalled " marble " or " alabaster," widely used by the peoples of the Gulf Coast region. Photograph courtesy of Peabody Museum, Harvard University.

ISLA DE SACRIFICIOS; Veracruz, Mexico   750-1000
Peabody Museum, Harvard University: C/7351   6 ¾ x 7 ¾ in.

68 *STONE PALMA*

Of the shorter type, this is quite different in proportion from that illustrated in Plate 75, and much less exuberantly carved. The design is that of a warrior wearing a face mask, from which a tongue protrudes.

VERACRUZ, Mexico   750-1000
Museum of the American Indian: 16/3473   H: 8 in.

69 *FIGURINE OF A YOUNG GIRL*

The appealing pose, simple costuming, and the effective facial modeling of this clay sculpture make this an outstanding example of Totonac art.

DICHA TUERTA; Veracruz, Mexico   300-600
Museum of the American Indian: 22/2310   H: 12 in.

70 *WOMAN HOLDING A FAN*

The coiffure, costuming, and jewelry of this superb large sculpture portray a matron of considerable importance. This may be an example of portraiture in clay.

LAS REMOJADAS; Veracruz, Mexico   300-900
Museum of the American Indian: 22/9277   H: 26 in.

71 *GIRLS IN A SWING*

This pair of lively young girls, painted red to indicate textile costuming, displays the sense of humor and life inherent in much of the early art of this region. These clay figures are actually whistles; each gives off a different tone when blown. The hair and headdress treatment shows something of the great variety of coiffures common at the time. Gift of John S. Williams.

EL FAISÁN; Veracruz, Mexico   300-600
Museum of the American Indian: 22/6374   6 x 6 in.

72 ARTICULATED FIGURINE

This sophisticated figurine effectively combines the techniques of mold-casting and hand-modeling to create a masterpiece; the fact that it was recovered with its limbs intact is even more remarkable. We do not know the function of these jointed figurines: perhaps they were puppets or children's dolls. However, the thin clay walls of the body are so fragile, it seems unlikely they ever had very much use. Gift of the Marion Eppley Memorial Fund.

JUACHÍN; Veracruz, Mexico
500-750

Museum of the American Indian: 23/735
H: 11 ¼ in.

73 STONE PALMA

This beautiful specimen is a fine example of the art of the Tajín period. The face presents a standing figure (perhaps *Xipe Totec*) with an elaborate head-dress, holding a staff. On the reverse side is a Corn Dancer, holding rattles shaped like ears of corn; he is reminiscent of the *Danzantes* at Monte Albán. This was originally in the collection of Governor Teodoro Dehesa of Veracruz. Photograph courtesy of the Nelson Gallery.

TEXOLO; Veracruz, Mexico   750-1250
Nelson Gallery, Atkins Museum: 49-47   H: 32 in.

74 ENGRAVED SHELL GORGET

Made from a section of giant conch shell, this beautifully carved object was once worn on the breast. The design, particularly characteristic of the Huástec people, is similar to that in Plate 46. The two coiled serpents, rising from the water, are balanced by elaborately costumed male and female figures. Photograph by Fred Zengel.

TAMPICO; Tamaulipas, Mexico   1000-1250
Middle American Research Institute: 35-688   4 3/16 x 7 7/16 in.

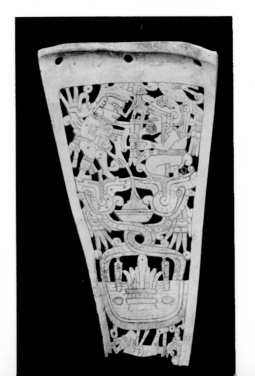

75 CARVED STONE YOKE

This is a classic example of the famous *yugos* from Middle America, concerning whose use there has been so much debate. The typical Tajín interwoven linear pattern is beautifully demonstrated on this example, seen from the top. Photograph courtesy of the American Museum of Natural History.

VERACRUZ; Mexico 750-1000

American Museum of Natural History: 30.2/3408 15 x 16 ½ in.

76 STANDING STONE FIGURE

This famous statue of an important Huástec personage or deity, combines two dissimilar treatments of the same subject. Whether this was an attempt to portray a life-and-death view, or the dual nature of many of the ancient deities, we cannot now determine. We do know that this form was popular, since several of these conical-capped statues are known from the region. Photograph courtesy of the Brooklyn Museum of Art.

SAN VICENTE TANCUYALUB; San Luís Potosí, Mexico 1000-1250

Brooklyn Museum of Art: 37.2897 H: 62 in.

77 MODELED PORTRAIT HEADS

This pair demonstrates the effect of time upon art concepts. The upper, from Palenque, was once painted in colors, all of which have disappeared, leaving only the sculpture. The lower, from Uxmal, is of essentially the same time period, but retains much more color. To the Mayan, this latter was the natural state of the art; our taste today prefers that sculptural qualities dominate. Strong color usually effaces and thus completely changes the artistic effect of such sculpture. Upper photograph by Ferdinand Anton.

PALENQUE; Chiapas, Mexico
UXMAL; Yucatán, Mexico   500-1000

National Museum of Anthropology, Mexico   H: 8 ½ in.
Museum of the American Indian: 8/1972

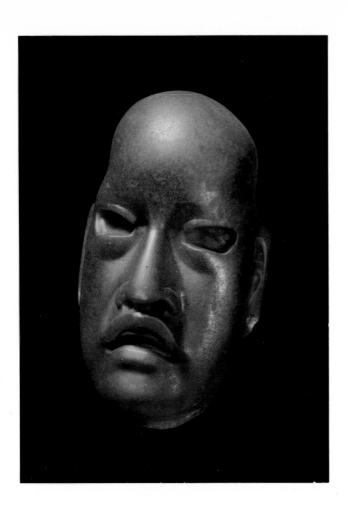

78 JADE HEAD FRAGMENT

The body of this classic Olmec head has been lost, but it remains a superb example of the art style from this horizon, one of the earliest yet established in Mexico. The perfection in technique and design makes it quite evident that these peoples had been working fine stone for many years; it was not a recently acquired skill. Collected about 1895 by Julius A. Skilton.

PALENQUE; Chiapas, Mexico   *ca.* 500 B.C.
Museum of the American Indian: 4/6274   H: 2 ¾ in.

79 CYLINDRICAL VESSEL

These hollow clay tubes are found throughout the Mayan area, particularly in Tabasco and Chiapas. They were used in funerary rites, perhaps as receptacles for sacrificial offerings. They were originally brightly painted, but few retain their color; the elaborate clay *appliqué* ornamentation is also rarely found intact. This example is unusual for its fine condition. The face is that of the Sun God, and the over-all design is symbolic of *Ik,* one of the Maya day signs. Photograph by Ferdinand Anton.

PALENQUE; Chiapas, Mexico   600-950
National Museum of Anthropology, Mexico   H: 45 ½ in.

80 *TRIPOD RATTLE VASE*

This fine orange ware vase is characteristic of a wide range of Mayan ceramics. Clay pebbles are inserted into the hollow bulbous legs, making this a musical instrument; this is a common technique in Mayan pottery—some bowls are known with false bottoms, in which clay pellets were placed prior to firing. Photograph courtesy of the Detroit Institute of Arts.

JAINA ISLAN; Campeche, Mexico   1000-1200
Detroit Institute of Arts: 63.39   H: 9 in.

81 *GROUP OF CLAY WHISTLES*

The great interest of these varied objects is not only their aesthetic merit, but the amount of information they give us as to the customs and daily life of the Mayan peoples. All are basically mold-made, and finished by hand-modeling; each is a whistle. The warrior carries a shield and club; the tall woman shows Mayan facial decoration and tattooing, and the elaborately costumed noble is apparently seated on a carved throne. The left whistle portrays a man, perhaps a hunter, wearing a *javelina* mask; it still retains much of its original blue paint.

JAINA ISLAND; Campeche, Mexico   700-1200
Museum of the American Indian: Tallest: 9 ¼ in.
    23/2860, 23/2861, 23/2274, 23/2862

82 STANDING WARRIOR FIGURINE

Elaborately costumed, carrying a feathered ceremonial shield, this modeled figurine demonstrates the dignified haughtiness so characteristic of Mayan art of this area. His face carries the marks of tattooing and head deformation practiced by these people. Photograph courtesy the Nelson Gallery.

GUAYMIL; Campeche, Mexico 900-1200
Nelson Gallery, Atkins Museum: 61-77 H: 12 ½ in.

83 STANDING FIGURE

Remarkable for the sensitive modeling of the face, the pensive pose, and the unusual size, this is truly a Mayan masterpiece. This bearded man, whose hair is caught in a skullcap of sorts and swirled in an effective loop, holds two pots in his left arm. Around his waist is a woven fiber belt and loincloth. At one time, this dramatic figurine was painted with blue and red paint, but most of this is now gone.

GUAYMIL; Campeche, Mexico 900-1200
Museum of the American Indian: 23/2573 H: 14 ½ in.

84 CARVED FEMUR BONE

This section of a human femur bone has been carved with elaborately interworked patterns, which are shown on the rolled-out impression in clay (*left*). The purpose of such objects is not known, although many of them have been recovered in excavations. Photograph courtesy of the American Museum of Natural History.

JAINA ISLAND; Campeche, Mexico   900-1200
American Museum of Natural History: T109/151   L: 5 ¹/₈ in.

85 PLUMBATE WHISTLING VESSEL

This effigy of the Fire God holding a bowl between his legs is superbly modeled in steel-gray plumbate. He is nestled in the heart of a conch shell—which can actually be blown as a trumpet. The bulbous supports are rattle legs, similar to those in Plate 80. See Plate 48. Gift of the Marion Eppley Memorial Fund.

GUAYMIL; Campeche, Mexico   900-1200
Museum of the American Indian: 23/900   9 x 9 ½ in.

86 MODELED CLAY URN

This elaborately modeled vessel portrays a priest, or nobleman, seated on a throne. While the costuming is relatively simple, the throne is a rococo assortment of decorative elements representative of feathers, carving and related adornments. This should be compared with similar objects in Plates 78 and 98 or 99. Photograph courtesy of the Instituto Nacional de Antropología e Historia.

TEAPA; Tabasco, Mexico   600-950
Regional Museum of Villahermosa, Tabasco   H: 23 7/8

87 CARVED WOODEN FIGURINE

This majestic seated figure in wood is the only such piece known from the Mayan area—proof of the tragic loss due to time and climate. The pose of the body, with its serene, curled-mustache features, and the cleanly detailed costuming all combine to give added support to arguments claiming Oriental origin or influence for much of this art. Photograph by Charles Uht; courtesy of The Museum of Primitive Art.

TABASCO; Mexico   600-1200
Museum of Primitive Art: 62.172   H: 14 in.

88 *PAINTED ORANGEWARE BOWL*

This shallow bowl is typical of the ceramics found in the Mayan regions of Mexico, and as far south as Guatemala and Honduras. The warm red-orange surface is decorated with various themes in black and red.

CAMPECHE; Campeche, Mexico   1200-1500
Museum of the American Indian: 23/102   D: 13 in.

89 *SEATED STANDARD BEARER*

This effigy is reminiscent of the recumbent *Chac Mool* carvings found in several regions of Mexico. The composition details are remarkably balanced; the facial features emerge from the shadows with tremendous power in this illustration. The slight costuming serves primarily to define the footwear of the period. Several of these figures once held wooden poles for banners, and were set up at the entrances of temples or palaces. Photograph by Ferdinand Anton.

CHICHÉN ITZÁ; Yucatán, Mexico   1000-1500
Regional Museum of Yucatán, Mérida   H: 30 in.

This ancient city of the Itzá people, perhaps one of the best known sites in Mexico, spreads over a tremendous area. The illustration gives some idea of the scope of the ruin, together with a general concept of the architectural layout of the various structures. Photograph by Ferdinand Anton.

CHICHÉN ITZÁ; Yucatán, Mexico · 455-1697

Founded as their capital by the Xiú, a tribe of Mayan invaders, the great site is well known to travelers today. This view shows the Palace of the Governors, House of the Turtles, Nunnery, and the Temple of the Magician. Mayan architectural layout and baroque ornamentation is clearly evident throughout. Photograph by Ferdinand Anton.

UXMAL; Yucatán, Mexico   500-1500

A fresco from the Toltec ruin situated high on the cliffs overlooking the Caribbean Sea. It portrays an elaborately costumed priest apparently placing a clay effigy on an altar. Just such effigies are shown in this volume; see Plate 105. Photograph by Ferdinand Anton.

TULUM; Quintana Roo, Mexico   500-1000

93 *CAVERN INTERIOR*

This photograph illustrates how many specimens were originally deposited. Although the arrangement has been slightly formalized, these bowls, Tlaloc vases, *manos*, and *metates* offerings are essentially as they were left, centuries ago. Photograph by Ferdinand Anton.

BALANCANCHÉ; Yucatán, Mexico   1000-1500

94 *MODELED MAYAPÁN URN*

Similar to those found at Mayapán, in Yucatán, and of the same type as that shown in Plates 45 and 86, this bears the effigy of an elaborately costumed priest. One hand has been lost; the orangeware clay retains much of the white paint once covering the figure, but the more colorful pigments are now gone.

SAN ANTONIO; Quintana Roo, Mexico   1200-1500
Museum of the American Indian: 8/1981   H: 21 ½ in.

95 *THE LITTLE PEOPLE OF MIDDLE AMERICA*

In an effort to show the humor and animation so frequently expressed in Middle American art, this group of clay figurines was arranged to present a view of " what might have been." All but one are from the Jalisco-Nayarit-Colima area, and date from the same general period.

As the women sit gossiping around a cooking pot,

a small urchin entertains a hunchbacked friend by blowing on a conch-shell trumpet. In his audience are a dancer, a fisherman, ball-players, acrobats, and a nobleman seated in a carrying chair.

A shaman, treating a sick patient, pays no attention to three warriors seated behind him; one of them, aroused by dogs barking at a snake, is about to

dispatch the reptile with a slingshot. A young girl
is serving tortillas to six customers gathered around
her, while costumed dancers perform for a visiting
Veracruz nobleman, wearing a mask and feathered
headdress. Photograph arranged by Alice W. Dockstader.

JALISCO-NAYARIT-COLIMA; Mexico   *ca.* 500-1250
Museum of the American Indian   Smallest: 1 in. Tallest: 7 in.

96 CARVED SHELL ORNAMENTS

This assortment presents a cross-section of the variety of design in shell carving. Most of these were personal decorations; a few were used for ornamenting objects or statues. The large central object is the wind symbol of *Quetzalcóatl*, and is often seen worn around the neck of personages representing that deity. It is made by cutting across the upper portion of a conch shell.

Mexico 750-1500
Museum of the American Indian Largest: 3 x 3 ½ in.

97 ECCENTRIC FLINTS

The reason for this name is obvious after a glance at the illustration; these were made in various sizes by Mayan artists, who used flint, chert, and obsidian for the purpose. They are found buried in cache-offerings scattered throughout the Mesoamerican region; similar objects are often seen in stela carvings, held in the hands of priests. These, from the collection of the Earl of Northesk, were presented by Harmon W. Hendricks.

Río Hondo; British Honduras 1000-1500
Museum of the American Indian: 13/5546, 13/5547 L: 14 in.

98 FUNERARY CYLINDER

Similar to the pottery tubes at Palenque in Plate 79, this grotesquely decorated example is in a quite different style, yet the over-all design demonstrates an interrelationship of the Mayan peoples of the two regions. The zoning, facial treatment, and use of the moan-bird make it obvious that the same Sun God symbolism is intended. This specimen, which retains much of its original paint, was collected by Thomas Gann about 1900. Gift of James B. Ford.

Cayo; British Honduras 500-1250?
Museum of the American Indian: 9/1819 H: 15 ½ in.

99 ORNAMENTAL STAFF HEAD

Carved from the axis of a giant conch shell, this bird effigy probably once graced the head of a wooden staff. Although there may have been inlays in the eye sockets at one time, no trace of these now remain. Full advantage has been taken of the natural form of the shell in this lovely carving. Photograph courtesy of the American Museum of Natural History.

WILD CANE CAY; Toledo, British Honduras 1000-1500
American Museum of Natural History: 30.0/2182 L: 9 in.

101 *CARVED JADE PENDANTS*

Of a form different from the style shown in Plates 58 or 139, these reflect the ability of the Indian lapidary to work his designs into a natural form without altering the stone. Into each shape, a deity wearing an elaborate headdress has been neatly accommodated; careful study reveals many costuming and iconographic details.

MAZATENANGO; Suchitepequez, Guatemala   300-600
Museum of the American Indian: Largest: 1⅝ in.
    15/3633, 15/3636, 15/3639, 15/3631

100 *GROTESQUE CLAY HEAD*

A fragment from a large urn, this baroque modeling was recovered at Lake Amatitlán in 1920 by Marshall H. Saville. It is typical of many which have been found more recently by skin-divers working in the same vicinity. Gift of James B. Ford.

LAKE AMATITLÁN; Amatitlán, Guatemala   500-800
Museum of the American Indian: 9/8508   H: 14¼ in.

Still another style of stone cutting is demonstrated in the four green steatite carvings illustrated. This particular combination is found nowhere else; the varieties of design and colorful stone make these small pendants extremely attractive. Gift of F. A. Mitchell-Hedges.

ROATÁN and MORAT; Bay Islands, Honduras   1000-1500

Museum of the American Indian: Largest 2 1/8 x 3 in.
     18/7694, 18/7691, 18/7699, 18/7631

This two-piece *incensario* retains much of its original color. The top lifts off to permit the depositing of copal in the base; smoke escapes through the perforations in the *guilloche* band around the forehead. Photograph courtesy of the University Museum.

CHIMUXÁN; Alta Verapaz, Guatemala   1000-1400

University Museum: 37-12-44   H: 9 1/2 in.

104 *HEAD OF A PRIEST*

Considerable interest is attached to this powerfully worked head not only for its aesthetic merit, but equally for the remarkable resemblance to Japanese *Nō* mask art. It was once tenoned into the wall of the great palace at Quiriguá, where it was collected by Marshall H. Saville in 1920. Gift of James B. Ford.

QUIRIGUÁ; Izabal, Guatemala   750-1000
Museum of the American Indian: 9/8199   H: 9 ½ in.

05 *SEATED EFFIGY FIGURINE*

Another two-part incense burner, this beautifully modeled effigy was found at Tikal. Representing an old man examining a frog which he holds in his hands, he wears an ornately decorated belt and headdress. Photograph by William R. Coe; courtesy of the University Museum.

TIKAL; El Petén, Guatemala   500-750
National Museum of Guatemala: 12C-508   H: 14 ¼ in.

106 *PLUMBATE EFFIGY JAR*

Apparently depicting an Owl Warrior, this modeled figure wears a costume with details reminiscent of Toltec and Aztec warriors in Mexico. He carries a shield similar to that shown in Plate 46. Photograph courtesy of the University Museum.

CHIPAL; El Petén, Guatemala   1000-1250
University Museum: NA 11531   H: 7 in.

107 *MOLDED VASE*

The banded decoration on the sides of this ovoid vase is, in a sense, a reversed design, indicating the use of molds in manufacture. The two eagle warriors are costumed in the elaborate feathered costumes of the period. Photograph courtesy of the University Museum.

EL QUICHÉ; Guatemala   600-900
University Museum: 12696   H: 7 ½ in.

108 CARVED STONE HACHA

This beautifully proportioned *hacha* showing a man wearing a zoömorphic headdress, is of the square form found more commonly in the Mexican area. Although it lacks the projecting tenon of the latter, it was used in much the same manner, presumably as an architectural ornament. See Plate 60.

SANTA LUCÍA COTZUMALHUAPA; Escuintla, Guatemala   500-750
Museum of the American Indian: 15/5708   7 ½ x 9 ¾ in.

109 CYLINDRICAL REDWARE URN

The appliqué design features a warrior in an eagle (or perhaps owl) helmet, carrying a dagger. Of a type quite different from the head fragment in Plate 100, this vessel minus its cover was recovered from the waters of the same lake around 1920. Surprisingly enough, it retains some of its original red, white, and green coloring. Collected by Mrs. J. Rodezno.

LAKE AMATITLÁN; Amatitlán, Guatemala   500-800
Museum of the American Indian: 12/3598   H: 10 ½ in.

110 PAINTED CLAY MASKETTE

The color on this delicately modeled maskette has been preserved in remarkable condition. The use of masks is less common in the middle and lower Mayan area than in Mexico, but it does extend as far south as Panama. Photograph by Alice W. Dockstader.

RÍO NEGRO; Alta Verapaz, Guatemala   1000-1500
National Museum of Guatemala: 55385   4 x 5 in.

111 DRUM-SHAPED BRAZIER

Similar in form to that shown in Plate 93, this cylindrical incenser has decorative motifs also reminiscent of Mexican art styles. The modeled figure on the side holds a shield in one hand, and an " eccentric flint " object in the other. One of a pair collected in 1919 by Marshall H. Saville. Gift of James B. Ford.

QUIRIGUÁ; Izabal, Guatemala   750-1000
Museum of the American Indian: 9/8467   H: 15 ½ in.

112 MUSHROOM STONE

Of unknown use, these are found widely distributed throughout Guatemala in particular. Many lack the figure carving, substituting a zoömorphic element or simply the tripodal "mushroom" effect. Presumably the concept relates to a narcotic cult known to have been prevalent in ancient Mesoamerica; there seems no phallic significance, as was earlier believed. Gift of James B. Ford.

MOMOSTENANGO; Totonicapán, Guatemala   500-1250
Museum of the American Indian: 9/8304   H: 13 in.

113 *SEATED FIGURINE*

Among the largest carved Mayan " jades," Foshag identifies this as muscovite, a micaceous mineral. At one time this superbly proportioned effigy had inlaid eyes, perhaps of shell. The tiny holes were for attaching gold or feather ornaments; traces of cinnabar coloring also remain. The carving technique, facial incising and over-all art style point to considerable Olmec influence. Photograph by Alice W. Dockstader.

UAXACTÚN; El Petén, Guatemala   250-500
National Museum of Guatemala: 921   H: 10 ¼ in.

114 *SCULPTURED ITZAMNÁ STELA*

Presumably a symbolic representation of the so-called "Long-Nosed God," this sinuously carved shaft was erected in front of a temple site. Attributed to *Itzamná*, one of the four sky gods, the face of the deity may be seen in profile in the center of the design. See Plate 146. Gift of Rodman Wanamaker.

SANTA CRUZ QUICHÉ; El Quiché, Guatemala   500-100 B.C.
Museum of the American Indian: 9/6718   H: 57 ¾ in.

115 *COVERED BLACKWARE DISH*

A beautifully finished bowl with modeled cover, this vessel bears a delicately incised decoration typical of many Mayan vessels of the period. The hollow panther-head ornament has an unusually life-like quality. Photograph courtesy of Peabody Museum, Harvard University.

HOLMUL; El Petén, Guatemala   500-1000
Peabody Museum, Harvard University: C/5572   9 1/2 x 13 3/8 in.

116 *PAINTED DISH AND COVER*

This beautiful vessel, excavated at Tikal in 1961, has an exuberantly painted parrot's-head handle. The coloring and iconography on the side of the dish is remarkably like fresco-decorated pottery from Teotihuacán. Photograph by William R. Coe; courtesy of the University Museum.

TIKAL; El Petén, Guatemala   750-1000
National Museum of Guatemala: 12C-546   D: 10 7/8 in.

117 *TRIPOD JAR AND COVER*

Also reflecting Teotihuacán influence, this blackware vessel bears an incised panel with what appears to be a duplication of the parrot-head cover ornament. Traces of cinnabar remain from the original coloring. Collected at Miraflores by Richard Stoeber before 1925.

KAMINALJUYÚ; Guatemala, Guatemala   200-500
Museum of the American Indian: 16/6235   H: 13 3/4 in.

118 *COVERED POLYCHROME BOWL*

The bowl of this brilliant orangeware vessel is severe, and contrasts with the careful elaboration of the modeled finial on the cover. Aside from the incised lines on the tripod supports, no other decoration is to be seen. Although said to have been recovered at Kaminaljuyú, this is of the form more common to the Petén region.

KAMINALJUYÚ; Guatemala, Guatemala   500-1000
Museum of the American Indian: 23/2217   H: 10 ¾ in.

119 *INCISED WARE EFFIGY*

An example of another early pottery technique is this human figure in brown clay. Often such incised patterns are colored by the addition of a dry pigment, such as cinnabar, lime, or the famous "Maya blue." Unfortunately, this color rarely survives the climate in which such objects were buried. Photograph by Ferdinand Anton.

KAMINALJUYÚ; Guatemala, Guatemala   250-750
National Museum of Guatemala   H: 9 in.

120 *ELABORATELY CARVED VASE*

Although this famous ceramic masterpiece has been the subject of considerable controversy, it has a long history, and bears up well under careful examination. It is unique, although a few somewhat similar vessels are known. It represents the work of a master Guatemalan ceramist, even though we may not be certain of the dating. Gift of Harmon W. Hendricks.

SAN AGUSTÍN ACASAGUASTLÁN; Zacapa, Guatemala   1500?
Museum of the American Indian: 20/7626   8 x 7 ½ in.

121 *CARVED STONE STELA*

Known as Stela 26, this is one of the best preserved such carvings found at Tikal. It was discovered inside of a tomb, which accounts for the excellent condition. Careful examination of the glyphs reveals many designs used by the ancient people in their communications symbology. Photograph by William R. Coe; courtesy of the University Museum.

TIKAL; El Petén, Guatemala   250-750
National Museum of Guatemala   H: 43 in.

122 *POLYCHROME OLLA*

Chinauhtla ceramics are representative of the last Mayan pottery period prior to the Conquest. This red-and-black decorated creamware olla is adorned with puma-head handles. Photograph by Alice W. Dockstader.

MIXCO VIEJO; Chimaltenango, Guatemala	1250-1500
National Museum of Guatemala: 6826	H: 12 in.

123 *POLYCHROME TRIPOD VASE*

This form, so favored by Mayan artists, also represents the peripheral art style. The *guilloche* band is common in El Salvador, as is the design on the lip of the vessel. The panel design apparently represents a serpent about to seize a warrior, who holds a shield in front of him. Photograph by Ferdinand Anton.

SAN SALVADOR?; El Salvador	500-1000
National Museum " David J. Guzmán," El Salvador	H: 8 ½ in.

124 *CYLINDRICAL VASE*

The parade of birds—cranes, or perhaps herons—
around the band at the top of this vessel replaces the
more usual glyphic design in such decorations. The
central panel is another view of a bird, or possibly
a symbolic representation of the Quetzalcóatl figure.
Although this brilliantly painted vase shows Mayan
influence, it also reveals the loss of much of the
understanding of Mayan iconography. Photograph by
Ferdinand Anton.

SAN SALVADOR?; El Salvador   500-1000
National Museum " David J. Guzmán," El Salvador   H: 6 ½ in.

125 *STONE HUNCHBACK EFFIGY*

These figurines are common to a limited area in the vicinity of San Salvador; usually carved from a porous material, they feature a circular perforation, seated posture, and coarse facial detail. Smooth-ground examples are less frequently seen.

SAN SALVADOR?; El Salvador   750-1250
Museum of the American Indian: 11/1309   5 ¼ x 7 ½ in.

126 *INCISED EFFIGY VESSEL*

The bridge between Costa Rica and Guatemala is evident in this anthropomorphic blackware vessel, since similar decorations are found in both areas. Photograph by Ferdinand Anton.

SAN SALVADOR?; El Salvador · 750-1000
National Museum " David J. Guzmán," El Salvador · H: 6 ½ in.

127 *MODELED HEAD EFFIGY VESSEL*

The careful incising suggests the linear decoration found in southern Mexico, but the suggestion of Mayan use of jade beads inserted under the skin makes it even more intriguing. The loops may have been intended for suspension, or possibly for the attachment of ornaments. Collected about 1900 by Ernest Schernikow.

SAN SALVADOR?; El Salvador · 500-1000
Museum of the American Indian: 3/3532 · 6 ¼ x 7 ¾ in.

128 *CARVED DEATH-HEAD HACHA*

The outline carving technique of this skull is found more frequently in Guatemala and El Salvador. At one time the eye was possibly inlaid, and there may have been a lower jaw, as suggested by the drilled depressions. Such separate lower mandibles are known in museum collections. Collected in 1924 by Samuel K. Lothrop.

CHILANGA; Morazán, El Salvador · 750-1000
Museum of the American Indian: 13/598 · H: 9 ½ in.

129 INCISED POLYCHROME VASE

With an incised decoration not unlike that in Plate
101, the lip of this vessel is typical of others from
the same area (Plate 142); the general form is that of
the whole sub-Mayan region. It was collected in 1919
during the excavation for the *Hospicio,* by Marshall
H. Saville. Gift of James B. Ford.

SAN SALVADOR; El Salvador   500-1000
Museum of the American Indian: 9/9572   6 ½ x 8 in.

130 STEATITE MASK

Stone masks are uncommon south of Guatemala; this
example is one of but two known from the Pipil area.
Carved from light-green steatite, it has the *guilloche*
design so popular in Pipil art. The string-sawing
technique used to separate it from the block shows
on the reverse. Collected in 1925 by Samuel K. Lothrop.

QUELEPA; San Miguel, El Salvador   250-750
Museum of the American Indian: 13/601   7 ¼ x 6 ¾ in.

131 CARVED STONE DISK

Known popularly as the *Disco Solar,* this portrayal of
a panther head with bared fangs seemingly has little
relationship to any Sun Deity usage. It is, however, a
reminder that powerful stone sculpture was not restricted to the more northerly Mayan area. Photograph by
Ferdinand Anton.

CARA SUCIA; Ahuachapán, El Salvador   1200-1500
National Museum " David J. Guzmán," El Salvador   D: 33 in.

136 *CARVED MARBLE VASE*

Among the loveliest of all prehistoric art objects from Middle America, these graceful containers originate in a small region in the Ulúa Valley, but have been found widely distributed, presumably through inter-tribal trade. Little is known of their iconography; Toltec influence is apparent in some, while Tajín-like designs are found in others. Their relationship to similar Chinese bronzes seems questionable. Photograph by Fred Zengel; courtesy Middle American Research Institute.

ULÚA VALLEY; Cortés, Honduras   750-1000
Middle American Research Institute: 38-58 $6\,^5/_8$ x $7\,^3/_8$ in.

137 POLYCHROME VASE

Bearing the unmistakable imprint of ceramic work common to the Mayan artists, this cylindrical vessel combines traits also found in the more southerly area. The repeated use of paired figures and the banded decoration make this an unusually well-designed masterpiece. Photograph by Ferdinand Anton.

LAKE YOJOA; Santa Barbara, Honduras   500-750

Middle American Research Institute: 35-6981   7 x 7 ½ in.

138 CARVED STONE STELA

The great ceremonial center at Copán is famous for the large number of magnificently carved stelae and other stone monuments. This, known as Stela D, portrays an elaborately costumed priest in feathered headdress; it represents the most florescent period of Mayan art. It stands 12 feet high. Photography by Ferdinand Anton.

COPÁN; Copán, Honduras   *ca. 735*

139 SEATED JADE FIGURINE

One of the largest Mayan carved jades, this is remarkable for the manner in which the ancient artist fit the design into the natural shape of the jade boulder; it weighs 5 pounds, 3 ounces. The art style is typically Late Classic period, with the flamboyant costuming and headdress of that era. It was collected about 1915 by Thomas Gann. Gift of Archer M. Huntington.

COPÁN; Copán, Honduras   750-1000
Museum of the American Indian: 10/9827   4 ½ x 7 ¾ in.

140 POLYCHROME TRIPOD VASE

Two priests with painted faces confront each other on this powerfully designed masterpiece. Wearing fanciful bird headdresses and dressed in serpent costumes, they are apparently engaged in a formal ritual. The serpent band decoration around the top replaces the more usual Mayan glyph decoration. Gift of Harmon W. Hendricks.

YUSCARÁN; El Paraíso, Honduras   500-750
Museum of the American Indian: 6/1259   7 ⅞ x 9 ¼ in.

141 *MODELED CLAY FIGURINES*

A distinctive type of effigy is found in the Playa de los Muertos area of northern Honduras, and is amongst the earliest dated objects yet found in the area. Less well-known than they should be, these carefully modeled objects are found in many styles, of which the quartet illustrated here forms a representative selection. The facial features are well detailed, but the costuming is less elaborated than in Mexico.

ULÚA VALLEY; Cortés, Honduras

Museum of the American Indian:
  4/3874, 18/3091, 4/3872, 7595

250-750 B.C.

Tallest: 5 in.

142 *GLOBULAR POLYCHROME BOWL*

The design on this graceful bowl depicts a group of
priests parading around the circumference, in a style
similar to, but not precisely like, that in Plates 123
and 140. The band of designs around the lip has no
glyphic content. Collected near Chamelecón in 1915
by J. E. Austin.

ULÚA RIVER; Cortés, Honduras   500-750
Museum of the American Indian: 4/3811   H: 6 in.

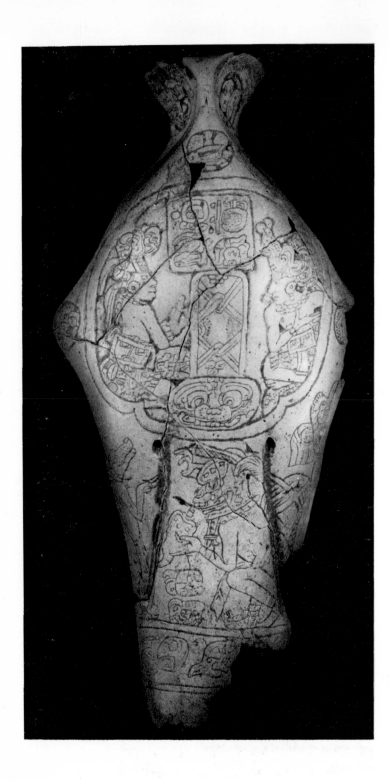

143 *INCISED PECCARY SKULL*

The two figures seated facing each other are carefully engraved onto the surface of this calvaria; the glyph panel records the Mayan date 9.7.8.0.0. The crouching Death God is flanked by peccaries and other animals. This is one of a pair discovered in Tomb 1 by George B. Gordon in 1896. Photograph courtesy of Peabody Museum, Harvard University.

COPÁN; Copán, Honduras *ca. 575*
Peabody Museum, Harvard University: C/201 L: 9 ½ in.

144 *KNEELING CLAY FIGURINE*

Of the same buffware composition as the figurines in Plate 141, this effgy is formed by the mold process, with details added by hand. It is smoother than most effigies from the Ulúa Valley region, and probably represents a slightly later period. The particular style of headdress is found throughout the central region of Middle America.

GRACIAS; Cortés, Honduras 100-250 B.C.
Museum of the American Indian: 6/1252 H: 7 ¾ in.

145 CROCODILE EFFIGY VESSEL

This grotesque covered effigy jar is similar to others from Nicaragua and Costa Rica. Commonly referred to as "alligator vessels," this may actually represent a *coati*, judging from the design. Modeled from dark-brown chocolate ware, it has the lumpy quality common to pottery in southern Central America. Gift of Francis E. Ross.

MANAGUA; Managua, Nicaragua   500-750
Museum of the American Indian: 23/3045   L: 10 ¾ in.

146 POLYCHROME TRIPOD BOWL

This brilliantly painted shallow bowl bears a design almost identical to the Long Nosed God on the stela in Plate 114. Although other parts of the decoration differ, there would seem little doubt the two portray the same individual—an example of the distribution of a similar religious concept. Gift of Francis E. Ross.

SAN ISIDRO; Granada, Nicaragua · 750-1250
Museum of the American Indian: 23/2120 · D: 6 ½ in.

147 STANDING CLAY FIGURINE

The style and proportions of this buffware figurine are related to others in El Salvador and Honduras, but the over-all concept is distinctively Nicaraguan. See Plate 151. Photograph by Ferdinand Anton.

MANAGUA; Managua, Nicaragua · 750-1000
National Museum of Nicaragua · H: 6 in.

148 POLYCHROME HUMAN EFFIGY

The bright tones of color have not been lost from this little figure, presented wearing a fancy costume. The great use of black and orange hues relates to much of the pottery from the southern Middle Americas; this example was collected on the shores of Lake Nicaragua about 1920 by Raúl R. Barrios.

RIVAS; Rivas, Nicaragua · 1000-1250
Museum of the American Indian: 15/9362 · H: 6 ¼ in.

149 *MONOLITHIC AX*

The graceful lines of this stone implement make it a worthy inclusion in a volume on prehistoric art. These are found in limited numbers throughout Middle America, but few are as cleanly carved and well-balanced as the example illustrated. Gift of David E. Harrower, who collected it on the mainland side of Bluefields lagoon, in 1925.

BLUEFIELDS; Zelaya, Nicaragua   750-1000
Museum of the American Indian: 13/2997   L: 12 in.

150 *ZOÖMORPHIC METATE*

This elaborately carved feline effigy was undoubtedly the prized possession of some wealthy individual; it seems unlikely that it was used for everyday purposes. These probably were employed in ceremonial corn-grinding rites, although nothing is known for certain of their use. See Plates 152 and 190. Gift of The Viking Fund.

MOYOGALPA; Ometepe Is., Nicaragua   1000-1500
Museum of the American Indian: 21/3798   8 ½ x 10 x 18 ½ in.

151 *PLAINWARE EFFIGY*

The brooding countenance, sleepy eyes and cleanly modeled features of this paunchy figurine suggest the artist intended it as a portrait, possibly humorous. The emphasis on the head rather than the balance of the figure is in keeping with many Middle American figurines. If there was ever any color on this specimen, it has been totally lost.

MANAGUA; Managua, Nicaragua   750-1000?
Museum of the American Indian: 23/2046   H: 9 ¼ in.

152 *ECCENTRIC CARVED METATE*

The involved forms in this fantastic design almost obscure the fact that it is a *metate*. Such ornate objects are rarely recovered intact; earth movement and excavation usually combine to break them up. This flying-panel example is a more elaborate example of the style illustrated in Plate 190. Photograph by Ferdinand Anton.

SAN ISIDRO GUADALUPE; Cartago, Costa Rica   1000-1250
National Museum of Costa Rica   H: 28 in.

153 *JAGUAR EFFIGY VESSEL*

This beautiful polychrome tripodal vase is typical of those excavated in Costa Rica and Nicaragua. The manner in which the bowl of the vessel has been made into the body form of the animal makes the whole design harmonious as well as functional. Even though the head is often grotesque, the over-all appearance makes these a distinguished part of any collection.

EL GENERAL; Puntarenas, Costa Rica   750-1000
Museum of the American Indian: 19/4896   H: 14 in.

154 *CARVED SERPENT DEITY*

This stone effigy crawling with snakes effectively presents one other style of Costa Rican sculpture. He holds a snake in each hand, another is suspended from his teeth, and two serpents are carved down his back. Three reptile heads peer over the top of the head of this figurine, whose identity is not known; we can only guess that he was a god figurine.

TURRIALBA; Cartago, Costa Rica   750-1000
Museum of the American Indian: 22/9580   H: 17 in.

155 *FEMALE EFFIGY*

Typical of the southern region of Costa Rica is this stiff, flat stone figure carved from a close-grained material. The triple-cut openings which form the limbs are most frequent in the Diquís style. Photograph courtesy Peabody Museum, Harvard University.

PALMAR SUR; Puntarenas, Costa Rica   1000-1500
Peabody Museum, Harvard University: 52-23-20/18948   H: 20 in.

156 POLYCHROME ATLANTEAN VASE

The exuberant color and fanciful modeling of Central American ceramics are shown at their best in this lovely specimen. The slender form with a bulbous base is supported by a crocodile standing on a ring— a form of support frequently seen in this region.

FILADELFIA; Guanacaste, Costa Rica   750-1000
Museum of the American Indian: 19/4981   H: 21 in.

157 CREAM-ON-REDWARE BOWL

Featuring another form of the popular "crocodile god" motif, this globular vessel of red-brown clay is decorated by a lively zig-zag pattern in cream-colored paint. This ware is scattered all through Highland Costa Rica; the present example was excavated in 1918 by Alanson B. Skinner.

ANITA GRANDE; Cartago, Costa Rica   1000-1500
Museum of the American Indian: 7/7337   H: 7 ¼ in.

158 SEATED POLYCHROME FIGURINE

The relationship of this specimen to that in Plate 148 is at once obvious. Although separated by many miles, the contemporaneity of the cultures and the similarity of the iconography points to a common background for the Nicarao and Chorotegan folk.

FILADELFIA; Guanacaste, Costa Rica   750-1000
Museum of the American Indian: 19/1416   H: 10 ½ in.

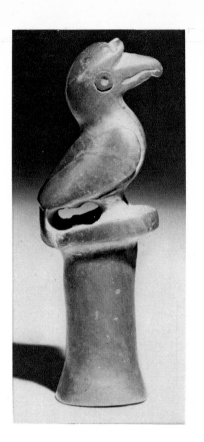

159 *CARVED STAFF HEAD*

In the form of a bird, this small greenstone object was presumably once the head of a wooden staff; it is drilled to allow the insertion of the shaft. The eye is inlaid with a red jasper bead. The technique of cutting the stone away beneath the body by drilling shows clearly in the photograph. Collected by Frank Squires in 1904.

Obispo; Guanacaste, Costa Rica　　　　　　750-1000
Museum of the American Indian: 1/2290　　　H: 2 ½ in.

160 *DEER-EFFIGY BOWL*

This tripod vessel apparently representing a deer is of low-fired biscuit ware, a delicately modeled pottery common in the Chiriquí region of Costa Rica and Panama. The extremely thin-walled bowl, with typically globular form, has legs with pebbles inserted to form rattles. Collected before 1900 by H. L. Cruikshank.

Río Chunque Viejo; Chiriquí, Costa Rica　　　1000-1500
Museum of the American Indian: 16/6007　　　H: 7 ¼ in.

161 *POLYCHROME FIGURINE*

This brightly hued little man, perhaps a *cacique* of the
Nicarao people, is made in the ceramic style typical
of the very early redware pottery found in the Nicoya
Peninsula. Photography by Ferdinand Anton.

Nɪᴄᴏʏᴀ; Guanacaste, Costa Rica   250-500
National Museum of Costa Rica   H: 5 in.

162 *CAST GOLD MUSICIAN*

The elaborate headdress worn by this tiny piper represents two huge feather plumes; his circular ear ornaments are often seen in the gold work of this general region. The bowl of his flute was crushed by the collapse of the tomb from which this 18 ct. pendant was collected by Frank Squires in 1904. Made by the lost-wax process, it weighs 125 grams.

CHIRIQUÍ; Costa Rica   1000-1500
Museum of the American Indian: 6262   H: 3 ¼ in.

163 STONE MACE HEADS

One of the unique art forms of the Costa Rican area is the manufacture of club heads, drilled to receive a round wooden shaft. Carved from several types of extremely hard stone, they are made in a tremendously wide range of designs.

NICOYA PENINSULA; Costa Rica   500-1000
Museum of the American Indian: Longest: 5 ¾ in.
    22/9577, 22/9579, 21/3427, 22/9575, 22/9578

164 CAST GOLD BELL

Formed in a single casting by the lost-wax process, this beautiful bell is ornamented by a carefully sculptured stag; it has a solid gold clapper. Such objects were commonly used on costumes, or fastened to staffs. Weighing 77 grams, this casting shows the masterful coupling of technical skill with esthetic taste.

LAS MERCEDES; Cartago, Costa Rica   1000-1500
Museum of the American Indian: 5/9849   H: 2 ¼ in.

165 *CARVED AX GODS*

This quartette shows in small scope the range of art styles as well as the development of a utilitarian form into an effigy representation. All are carefully cut, incised, and polished to a high luster; the cutting clearly shows the use of cords, whence the term "string sawing."

Nicoya Peninsula; Costa Rica   750-1250
Museum of the American Indian: Longest: 5 ¾ in.
    23/93, 23/2045, 22/4596, 7/4270

166 *RATTLE-LEG TRIPOD URN*

A major feature in Central American ceramic art is the wide range of designs which employ slit hollow legs, into which solid clay pebbles have been inserted, to form a rattle. In the present example, the majestic redware form of the urn dominates the design, but the legs are sufficiently strong to provide ample balance.

Línea Vieja; Cartago, Costa Rica   1000-1500
Museum of the American Indian: 15/8689   10 x 16 ½ in.

167 *MONOLITHIC CROCODILE GOD*

This great figure is characteristic of some of the huge sculpture from this region. It depicts a being usually called the "Crocodile God," who has a trophy head suspended from a cord around his neck. The missing arm probably once held an axe or a stone-headed club. Photograph courtesy of Brooklyn Museum of Art.

Palmar; Puntarenas, Costa Rica   1000-1500
Brooklyn Museum of Art: 34.5084   H: 60 in.

168 *PAINTED PEDESTAL VASE (TOP)*

The illustration is presented as looking down on the surface of the delicate designing of Panamanian ceramic painting. The representation is that of the Crocodile God, a favorite subject in Isthmian art.

SANTIAGO; Veraguas, Panama · 1000-1500
Museum of the American Indian: 22/8374 · D: 9¾ in.

169 *DEER EFFIGY BOWL*

A coarse brown ware, gritty in composition, and only mildly modeled, is characteristic of most of the pottery from Veraguas. This example is apparently in the form of one of the deer once common in the interior. Gift of Dr. and Mrs. Frederick J. Dockstader.

LAS FILIPINAS; Veraguas, Panama   1000-1500
Museum of the American Indian: 22/5954   H: 7 in.

170   *BIRD PEDESTAL BOWL*

This beautifully painted vessel is typical of Panama, and dramatically illustrates the pedestal form from that area. The body of the bird, perhaps a vulture, forms a container. This buffware usually loses much of its paint in the soil, such finely decorated examples are rare.

PARITA; Veraguas, Panama   1000-1500
Museum of the American Indian: 22/8374   H: 9 in.

171   *VULTURE EFFIGY BOWL*

Featuring a modeled vulture crouching over the globular bowl of the vessel, this painted design represents the circular pattern more ofen found in Coclé. Photograph by Francis E. Ross.

VERAGUAS, Panama   1000-1500
National Museum of Panama: 4-14-1962   13 x 16 in.

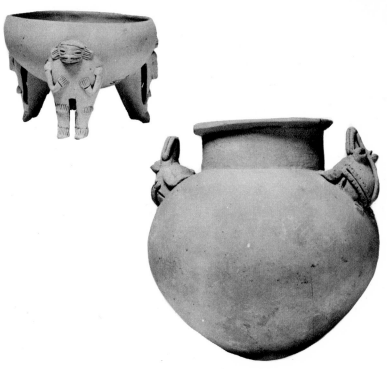

172   *BISCUITWARE VESSELS*

Characteristic of southern Costa Rica and northern Panama is an extremely thin-walled pottery, delicately tooled and beautifully modeled in a great variety of forms. These small *adornos* show a strong relationship to the cast gold work of the same area. Although this ware is almost never painted, it is extremely graceful and attractive. Gift of Minor C. Keith.

DIVALÁ; Chiriqui, Panama   500-1000
Museum of the American Indian: 4/3188, 3/6214   H: 6½ in.

179   CROCODILE GOD ORNAMENT

A remarkable form of gold decoration was common in
southern Middle America in the lost-wax process. The
usual form was of a human, animal, bird or mythological creature. Wide flaring extensions were placed at
either end, often decorated with snake (or crocodile)
heads. A ring was cast on the back for suspension on
the breast. It weighs 54 grams.

BOCAS DEL TORO; Chiriquí, Panama   1000-1500
Museum of the American Indian: 8242   L: 2 ¾ in.

180   CAST GOLD FIGURINE

This little man holding a rattle in one hand is
doubtless a musician wearing a ceremonial headdress.
Made from 22 k. gold by the lost-wax technique,
the amusing ornament weighs 30 grams; it was most
probably a pendant. Collected by F. D. Utley in 1906.

DIVALÁ; Chiriquí, Panama   1000-1500
Museum of the American Indian: 8267   H: 2 ½ in.

181 *ANTHROPOMORPHIC DESIGN (TOP)*

The humor so frequently seen in much of the Middle American ceramic art is nowhere more evident than in the work of the Panamanian artists. This happy design may have been intended to frighten the ancient folk, but to contemporary viewers it would seem more likely to have been created to amuse children. Photograph by Francis E. Ross.

Coclé; Panama	500-1000
National Museum of Panama: 4-14-1962	D: 11 in.

182 *HAMMERED GOLD DISK*

One of the most effective gold techniques in Middle America was the use of huge sheets of gold, incised and embossed with mythological designs. This example depicts the Crocodile God, with two accompanying beings. Pierced for suspension on the breast, they were found placed on the bodies or in the graves of important personages. This example weighs 169.5 grams. Photograph courtesy of Brooklyn Museum of Art.

Sitio Conte; Coclé, Panama	1000-1500
Broklyn Museum of Art: 33.48	8 1/2 x 9 in.

183 *POLYCHROME BURIAL URN*

This large vessel with four loop handles is of a type rarely found in Panama. The remarkable design is unlike most pottery designs in Chiriquí, even though the color, clay work and brush style are typical. Less than a dozen are known, and their dating is only conjectural. Gift of Peter J. Potoma, Jr.

TABASARÁ RIVER; Chiriquí, Panama   500-1000?
Museum of the American Indian: 22/9301   14 x 17 in.

184 GOLD ORNAMENTS

This trio of decorations from Coclé shows the great diversity found in that limited area. They were excavated by Samuel K. Lothrop in 1930-1933, and represent the fine technical skills of the ancient Panamanian goldsmiths. The alligator is cast by the lost-wax process, as is the two-headed zoömorphic bell; the ornamental nose ornament is repoussé work. Photograph courtesy Peabody Museum Harvard University.

SITIO CONTE; Coclé, Panama   1000-1500
L: Alligator, 4 ½ in. Bell, 3 x 4 in.
Peabody Museum, Harvard University:
193000, C/10679, C/11057

185 CROCODILE GOD BOWL

This magnificent vessel depicts the Crocodile God in pottery form. Painted in black and red on a buffware base, it has a powerful visual impact. Compare with Plates 176 and 179.

VERAGUAS, Panama   1000-1500
Museum of the American Indian: 22/9500   H: 9 ¾ in.

186 PAINTED PEDESTAL VESSEL

This peculiar form is more common in Panama, although it is found in several areas of America. Many of the illustrations in this volume are of the elaborately painted tops of these vessels (e.g., Plates 176 and 178). This, with seven zoömorphic heads, shows the manner in which the base was decorated. If the lip design is significant, there was apparently a "right and wrong" side to such objects.

VERAGUAS; Panama   1000-1500
Museum of the American Indian: 22/9512   9 x 10 in.

187 *INCISED SHELL ORNAMENT*

This spectacular mother-of-pearl ornament reflects the
same design style seen in many Coclé ceramic objects
(Plate 182). It was drilled for suspension, presumably
for use as a pendant.

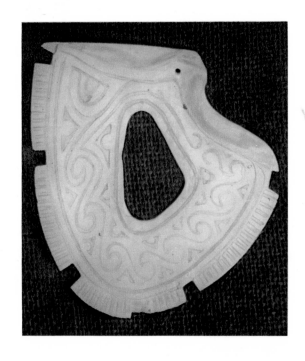

VENADO BEACH; Canal Zone, Panama   500-750

Museum of the American Indian: 22/5271   L: 5 in.

188 STONE BURIAL SHAFT

Stone columns of this style were carved and set up in the great cemetery on the flats along the Río Caño, perhaps as gravestones are used today. When found, most had fallen over; this was still erect. It apparently depicts a monkey eating; the reverse is carved to complete the body form. Excavated by A. Hyatt Verrill in 1926.

PENONOMÉ; Coclé, Panama   750-1500
Museum of the American Indian: 14/6217   L: 46 in.

189 CARVED WOODEN SEAT

The *duho,* a form of back-rest used by important persons throughout the West Indies, is found in many forms, often with carved features of animals or humans. These high-backed seats are apparently an intrusive item of furniture from northern South America.

TURKS ISLAND; Bahamas   1250-1500
Museum of the American Indian: 5/9385   L: 33 ½ in.

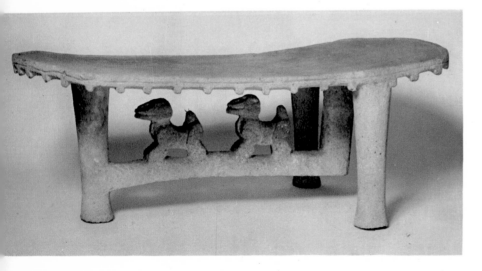

190 FLYING PANEL METATE

So called because of the free-form carving beneath the table, this tripod grinding-tablet is not as exuberant as that in Plate 152; however, it bears a resemblance to the many types of *metates* found in lower Middle America. This, with two animals, also has the tiny carved heads along the rim so frequently seen in Nicoyan and Chiriquían stone *metates*. Gift of Peter J. Potoma, Jr.

SANTIAGO; Veraguas, Panama   500-1000
Museum of the American Indian: 22/9431   14 ½ x 10 ½ x 30 in.

191 *SHELL CARVINGS*

This trio demonstrates the love for shell, and skill at carving, which was the pride of many West Indian artists. The tiny head is a pendant from Baracoa, Cuba; the conical cap of unknown function was excavated on Montserrat, while the recumbant figurine is a charm from Santo Domingo. Gift of Mrs. Wyllys Terry, Jr.

TAINO; West Indies   1000-1500
Museum of the American Indian: Longest: 2 ½ in.
   4/6037, 17/5076, 20/621

192 *STONE PESTLES*

The variety of pestles from the West Indies is enormous. These three demonstrate the animal and human forms most commonly seen, and represent the rounded carving favored by the Taino and Ciboney artists.

DOMINICAN REPUBLIC and PUERTO RICO   1000-1500
Museum of the American Indian: Longest: 7 ½ in.
   12/7424, 3/6314, 15/768

193 *HUMPBACKED CLAY IDOL*

The brooding cast to the countenance of this crouching figure gives it an atmsophere only augmented by the powerful modeling. It is one of the finest clay objects known from the West Indies. The incised decoration should be compared with Plate 198, and the extremely thin walls make this an amazing *tour de force* in ceramic art. It was set up on an altar in a cave where it was found by Theodoor de Booy in 1916.

ANDRÉS; Santo Domingo, Dominican Republic   1000-1500
Museum of the American Indian: 5/3753   H: 16 in.

194 *BUFFWARE WATER VESSEL*

The globular shape of this vessel has beautiful symmetry, and the slight touch of decoration at the neck of the vertical spout provides all the ornamentation needed. A fine example of restraint in ceramic art, it was collected in 1913 by Theodoor de Booy in the Salado Caves.

MACAO; La Altagracia, Dominican Republic   1000-1500
Museum of the American Indian: 3/3981   H: 18 in.

195 *INCISED POTTERY BOWL*

The staring gargoyle heads, or *adornos,* which decorate this vessel are indications of the spread of Taino influence into the eastern part of this island. The ware is almost identical to that found in neighboring Hispaniola and Puerto Rico. This bowl was found in a cave near Monte Cristo in 1915 by M. R. Harrington.

BARACOA; Oriente, Cuba   1000-1500
Museum of the American Indian: 4/1851   5 x 8 ½ in.

196 BONE FIGURINES

The two miniature effigies reveal the pervading sense of death which colors so much of Taino art. The smaller carving, from Puerto Rico, was intended as a pendant; the larger, from the Dominican Republic, may have been used as a staff-head. It was collected in 1908 by Adolfo de Hostos. Gift of Frederick J. Dockstader.

TAINO; West Indies   1000-1500
Museum of the American Indian: 23/2049, 1/9711   Tallest: 3 in.

197 CARVED SHELL ORNAMENTS

Typically Taino in form and design, these two carvings also feature the death's head motif so common to the region. The tiny figurine is drilled, presumably to accommodate a suspension cord. The maskette was apparently intended as a pectoral; there may have been inlay in the eyes at one time. Photograph courtesy of International Business Machines Corporation.

PUERTO RICO   1000-1500
University of Puerto Rico Museum: 38A   L: 4 ¼ in.
Museum of the American Indian: 31992   H: 2 in.

198 STONE "COLLAR"

This name became attached to this and similar carvings, earlier mistaken for collars. They may be belts, somewhat like the stone yokes from Mexico (Plate 75); they will fit over the hips, and can be worn more or less comfortably. The design should be compared with the belt design of the figure in Plate 193.

PUERTO RICO   1000-1500
Museum of American Indian: 1/6662   11 x 18 in.

199 *STONE ZEMI CHARMS*

These finely worked objects, whose function is completely unknown, are believed to have had a ceremonial use. The tri-pointed stone carving, commonly termed a *zemi*, has various forms, and usually the head of a human or animal adorns the ends. Collected by Jesse Walter Fewkes and Felix Seijo.

ARECIBO; Arecibo, Puerto Rico   1000-1500
Museum of the American Indian: Longest: 7 ½ in.
   3/1976, 19/917, 3697

200 *BASALT STONE SKULL*

An example of unusually powerful sculpture from any point of view, this *zemi* is a magnificent accomplishment of the ancient Taino artist. It was apparently intended for attachment to a staff; the ridges to hold the lashings can be seen at either end of the object. Photograph courtesy International Business Machines Corporation.

SAN PEDRO DE MACORIS; Dominican Republic   1000-1500
University of Puerto Rico Museum: 218A   4 x 7 ½ in.

201 *INCISED CLAY BOWL*

The grotesque decoration on the lip of this vessel is typical of the sub-Taino ceramic work. These gargoyles are found in tremendous numbers, almost always separate from the bowl they once adorned. The clay is of such poor quality that whole vessels are extremely rare; this example was recovered from caves on the island of La Gonâve in 1916 by Frank Crumbie, Jr.

LA GONÂVE; Haiti 1000-1500
Museum of the American Indian: 19/8852 7 x 13 in.

202 *BIRD-SHAPED VESSEL*

The peculiar pottery vessel is reminiscent of the " shoe pots " found all along the Middle American mainland. The tiny bird or animal modeling on the surface provides an attractive decoration. Collected in 1915 by Thomas Huckerby.

TRINIDAD; British West Indies 1000-1500
Museum of the American Indian: 4/592 H: 3 ½ in.

203 *GROUND STONE AXES*

One of the most remarkable qualities in West Indian art is the strong feeling developed by these people for stone, as this selection of ax heads eloquently demonstrates. These are worked from a hard, fine-grained stone after weeks of grinding and polishing. The group illustrated came from St. Vincent, Grenada and Guadaloupe.

TAINO; West Indies 1000-1500
Museum of the American Indian Longest: 12 in.

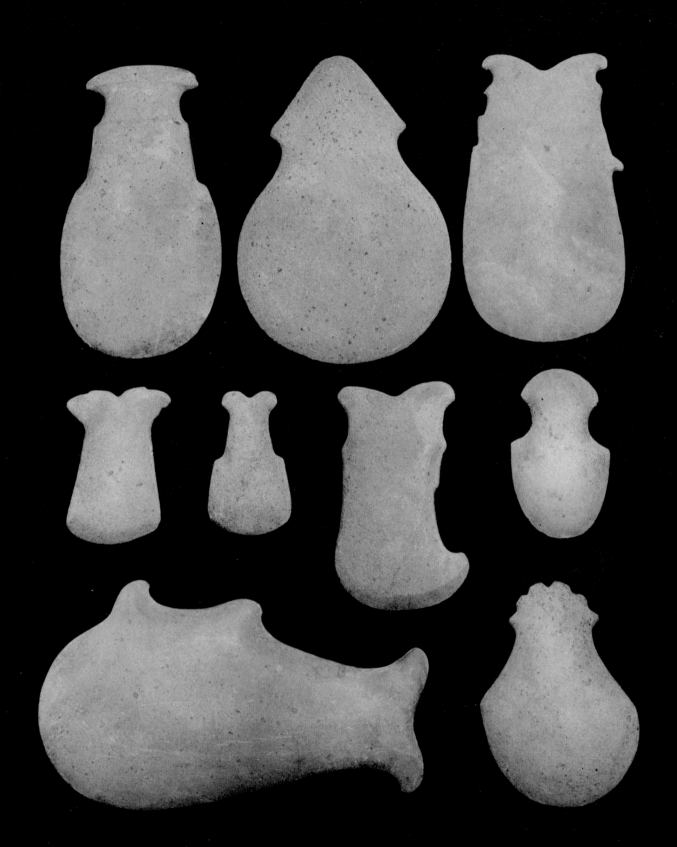

204 _ANTILLEAN STONE CARVINGS_

The intriguing variety in stonework common to the
Antilles is illustrated by this group of objects, whose
functions are not understood. The comma-shaped
specimens, thin-bladed and unperforated, are smooth
on both sides. The balance are recognizable zoömorphic forms of tufa. Such carving have a wide
distribution throughout the eastern West Indies.

Museum of the American Indian: 1000-1500
    _2/7739, 5/3422, 2/9967, 3/2015_   Longest: 9 in.

205 _SQUATTING STONE FIGURINE_

This small carving of mottled green-and-white serpentine was intended to be used as a pendant; a small
hole is drilled laterally through the shoulders. The
Lucayan sub-decorative style suggests similarities with
Taino objects in the more southerly Antilles. Collected
in 1910 by Theodoor de Booy.

Kew; North Caicos, Bahamas   1000-1500
Museum of the American Indian: 3/2200   H: 4 ¾ in.

206 ANTHROPOMORPHIC CARVING

The manner in which the aboriginal artist could take an ordinary oval rock and make a work of art from it is demonstrated in this simple carving. The low-relief technique is identical to many petroglyphs found scattered throughout Puerto Rico and Hispaniola. Gift of Mrs. Thea Heye.

SANTO DOMINGO; Dominican Republic   1000-1500
Museum of the American Indian: 16/5511   L: 4 ¼ in.

207 MODELED REDWARE SPOUT

A fragment from a larger vessel, this zoömorphic effigy is a large spout with a design commonly seen in the work of the Igneri people who lived south of Puerto Rico. It was collected in 1921 by Thomas Huckerby.

CARRIACOU; Grenada, British West Indies   1000-1500
Museum of the American Indian: 10/5163   H: 9 ½ in.

208 *SCULPTURED WOODEN IDOL*

Another form of the *zemi,* this menacing effigy with inlaid shell teeth represents the most traditional design style of the Taino folk. Such objects are among the rarest of West Indian sculptures; those which escaped the Spanish priests usually fell prey to the inhospitable climate. Photograph by Charles Uht; courtesy of the Museum of Primitive Art.

JAMAICA; British West Indies   1000-1500
Museum of Primitive Art: 56.180   H: 27 in.

209 COIL-WEAVE BASKET

These shallow baskets are woven in many striking patterns from strips of buff-colored *torote*. The contrast is provided by dying the fibers reddish-brown. The tightly woven coils give these carrying baskets tremendous strength. Collected at Kino Bay in 1930 by Dane Coolidge.

SERI; Sonora, Mexico   1925-1930
Museum of the American Indian: 20/3203   D: 16 in.

210 BOWL BASKET

Of the same technique as the following example, baskets of this shape are usually intended as storage containers. The stepped design makes a pleasing, rhythmic pattern. Collected on Tiburón Island in 1927 by Edward H. Davis.

SERI; Sonora, Mexico   1925-1930
Museum of the American Indian: 15/1247   H: 12 in.

211 *BEARDED DANCE MASK*

Carved from a very light wood painted dark brown, this mask has a design relationship to the *Pascolero* mask in Plate 212, and is used in similar ceremonies. The oval shape is given pleasing balance by the long horsehair beard and eyebrows. Collected at Sahuaral by Donald B. Cordry.

MAYO; Sonora, Mexico   1925-1940
Museum of the American Indian: 19/7741   Mask: 8 in.
                                              Beard: 8 in.

212 *CARVED PASCOLERO MASK (COLOR)*

Worn in annual Easter ceremonies, these attractively designed masks are elaborately painted and decorated for use by the *Pascola* dancers. Sometimes they are not worn in front of the face, but on one side of the head. The beard and eyebrows are of horsehair. Collected at Caborca about 1920 by Joseph Menager.

YAQUI; Sonora, Mexico   1915-1925
Museum of the American Indian: 10/2076   Mask: 7 in.
                                              Beard: 8 in.

213 *COTTON CARRYING BAGS*

A tremendous variety of pouches are woven by the Cora and Huichol Indians for decoration, and for carrying personal possessions. These illustrate two of the more frequent designs; colors are usually white and brown, or white and indigo. A long strap is used for suspension from the shoulder. Collected in 1923 by Edward H. Davis at Mesa del Nayar.

CORA; Nayarit, Mexico   1920-1925
Museum of the American Indian: 11/9388, 11/9405   11 x 11 in.

214 *WOVEN WOOL BELTS*

These four textiles are examples of the various belt designs most popular among the major weaving tribes of Mexico. Each is produced in varying colors, but follows a more-or-less standard pattern.

HUICHOL; Nayarit, Mexico   1925-1950
MIXTEC; Oaxaca, Mexico
TARAHUMARA; Chihuahua, Mexico
CORA; Jalisco, Mexico   Largest: 6 x 40 in.

Museum of the American Indian:
19/5379, 22/1421, 16/5263, 19/1973

215 *YARN "GOD'S EYE"*

These beautifully woven reed wands are used in the *Wimákwari* (Green Squash) Festival, held in October. The angular design represents the vehicle by which the god *Kauyumáli* sees and understands the world mysteries. The wand, called *síkuli,* constitutes a prayer that the eye of the god will see the supplicant; in the *Wimákwari* it is used to assure health and long life for children. This weaving technique is known throughout the Western Hemisphere. Collected in 1936 at El Cordón, by Donald B. Cordry.

HUICHOL; Nayarit, Mexico   1935-1940
Museum of the American Indian: 19/7856   L: 18 in.

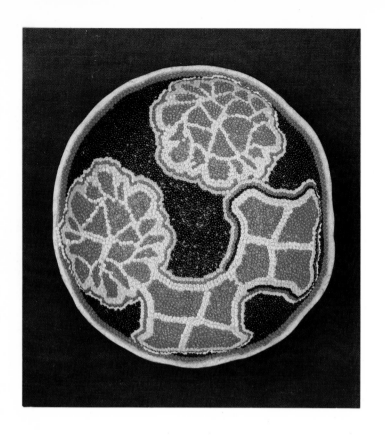

216 *BEADED GOURD BOWL*

Such bowls, decorated with beads, yarn, coins or many other objects, are used as prayer-offerings, and are deposited in small temples or at shrines. This is a contemporary example of a custom which has persisted for centuries. Made at Santa Caterina in 1962; collected by Frederick J. Dockstader.

HUICHOL; Jalisco, Mexico   1962
Museum of the American Indian: 23/2010   D: 8 ½ in.

217 *BEADWORK BRACELET*

Blue and white beads, obtained from traders, are woven in a variety of designs into bracelets, eardrops and other ornaments to beautify the person. Collected by Donald B. Cordry at El Cordón.

HUICHOL; Nayarit, Mexico   1935-1940
Museum of the American Indian: 19/9652   3 x 7 in.

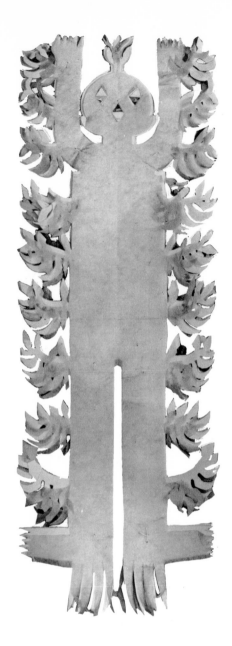

218 *COTTON POUCH*

Another example of the ubiquitous carrying pouch is this delicately woven shoulder bag, characteristic of the central region of Mexico. See Plate 213. Collected in 1930 at Toluca by Mrs. Howard M. Morse.

Oтomí; Querétaro, Mexico   1925-1935
Museum of the American Indian: 19/925   13 ½ x 14 ½ in.

219 *BARK-PAPER EFFIGY*

Such figures, representing a female deity, are placed in gardens to insure good crops. They are cut from sheets of hand-made paper pounded from the inner bark of the black mulberry tree. This example was collected at San Pablito about 1935. Presented by Miss Bodil Christensen.

Oтomí; Puebla, Mexico   1930-1940
Museum of the American Indian: 19/5165   L: 12 in.

A typical feature of these textiles is the seam uniting the two halves. Since the aboriginal loom is of limited width, the two strips are woven to fit, then sewn together; the test of the weaver's skill is the degree to which the elements of the design join along the seam. Collected in 1918 by George H. Pepper.

ZAPOTEC; Oaxaca, Mexico   1900-1920
Museum of the American Indian: 1/1925   55 x 75 in.

221 *BLACKWARE COLANDER*

This beautifully proportioned sieve is typical of a wide variety of unpolished pottery from Oaxaca; the rich black luster is obtained by exposing the clay to a smoke smudge during the firing process. From San Bartolo Coyotepec, this vessel was collected in 1962 by Frederick J. Dockstader.

ZAPOTEC; Oaxaca, Mexico   1960-1962
Museum of the American Indian: 22/5178   H: 10 ½ in.

222 *WOVEN SHOULDER BLANKET*

As with the textile in Plate 220, this blue-and-white *serape* is made by uniting two separately woven halves; a hole is usually left in the center to allow it to be slipped over the wearer's head. Of a later type, it shows the beginnings of outside influence, and from this central medallion style developed the contemporary designs featuring "Aztec Sun Calendars" and other more realistic patterns. Collected in 1920 by Mrs. Thea Heye.

ZAPOTEC; Oaxaca, Mexico   1920
Museum of the American Indian: 10/6813   40 x 60 in.

223 *WOMAN'S EMBROIDERED BLOUSE*

Although this might more accurately be termed " folk art," it is included to indicate the transition from indigenous to derived design; it clearly betrays the European influence in both decoration and cross-stitch technique. A clear-cut definition is difficult to establish, for the basic cut is that of the ancient *huipil*, which goes back to pre-contact times. See Plate 226.

MIXTEC; Oaxaca, Mexico   1900-1925
Museum of the American Indian: 10/938   29 x 35 in.

224 *JAGUAR MASK*

A modern example of the animal masking-complex so common to the pre-Columbian Indian, this *tigre* mask represents *Coh,* the Jaguar, and is worn in the Baile de Tun. While such masks are also made for the tourist trade today, they serve the Indian market equally. Presented by The Viking Fund.

QUICHÉ MAYA; El Quiché, Guatemala   1920-1960
Museum of the American Indian: 21/1008   7 x 8 ½ in.

225 *REDWARE BIRD EFFIGY BOWL*

This gracefully modeled vessel from San Luís Jilote-peque is an example of contemporary ceramic art which carries the pre-Columbian tradition in style and form up to the present. Photograph by Alice W. Dockstader.

QUICHÉ MAYA; Jalapa, Guatemala   1953
National Museum of Guatemala: 55329   L: 9 in.

226 *BROCADED COTTON BLOUSE*

Woven of unbleached native cotton, this richly decorated *huipil* shows Highland weaving at its best. Comparison with Plates 228 and 229 demonstrates the variety of textile patterns in these garments. Collected at Santo Tomás Chichicastenango in 1931 by Edith B. Ricketson.

Quiché Maya; El Quiché, Guatemala	1925-1931
Museum of the American Indian: 18/1100	29 x 35 in.

227 *CARVED WOODEN MASKS*

This selection shows the variety of Quiché Maya masks and the degree of European influence obvious in their design. These are used in the Bull Dance, Deer Dance, and Dance of the Conquest, which combine both pagan and Christian practice. Although wholly Indian used, they are carved by *mestizos,* and perhaps more properly fall within the category of folk art; they are included here to indicate the complexity of contemporary Indian art. Gifts of James B. Ford and Aaron Furman.

El Quiché; Guatemala	1875-1925
Museum of the American Indian:	Average: 7 x 8 in.
21/8635 (A Spaniard)	
22/7863 (A bull)	
14/5622 (Hernán Cortés)	

A magnificent embroidered garment, woven by a Cakchiquel woman to indicate her status in the village. Such beautifully made costumes are becoming less common as Europeanized dress is increasingly substituted in these villages. Collected in 1927 at Comalapa by Dr. Samuel K. Lothrop. See Plate 226.

MAYA; Chimaltenango, Guatemala 1920-1927
Museum of the American Indian: 16/950 22 x 39 in.

Other varieties of contemporary Highland textiles include this *perraje* (shawl) from San Pedro de la Laguna, showing how designs can be achieved from the tie-and-dye technique. The three *huipil* weaves are comparable to those in Plates 226 and 228. Two from Quezaltenango feature the rich brocading of that area as applied to the gauze weave and the plain cotton background material. The lower, from Mixco, is of the characteristic zigzag pattern found in Chimaltenango.

Sololá, Quezaltenango, and Chimaltenango, Guatemala 1920-1930
Museum of the American Indian: 18/1113, 16/609, 16/621, 16/540

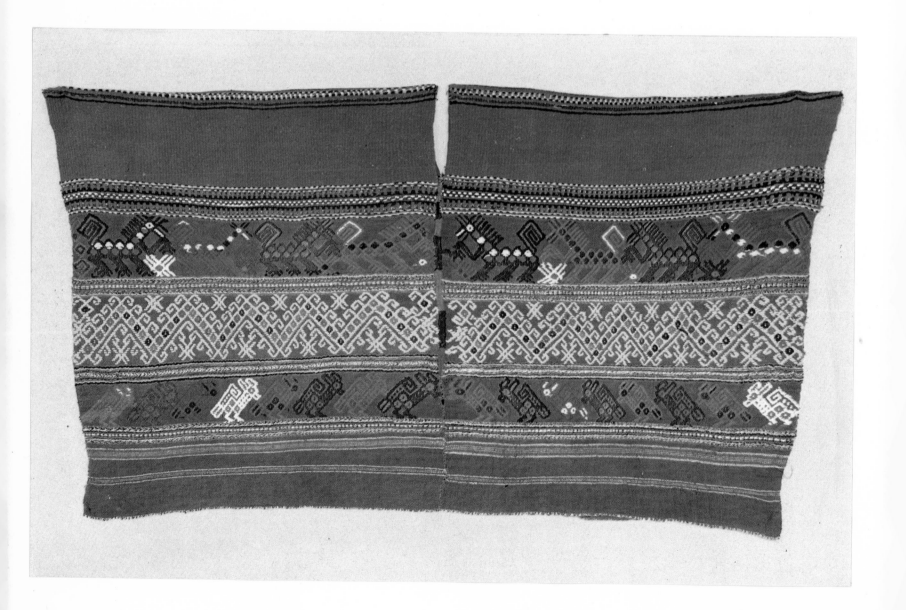

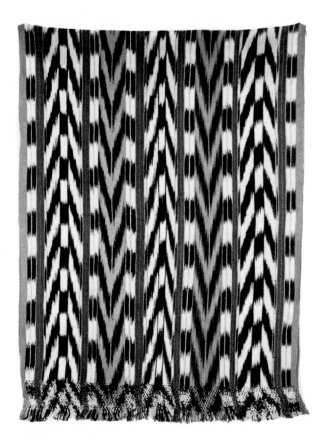

230 *COTTON DRESS YARDAGE*

Hand woven by the tie-dye technique, this is representative of the thousands of yards of weaving turned out regularly, almost solely for Indian customers. Most of this will be used in women's skirting, the colors and design indicating the wearer's locale. This specimen from Sonsonate is a basic brown, with designs in red, yellow, and white. Collected in 1924 by Samuel K. Lothrop.

LENCA; Ahuachapán, El Salvador   1920-1924
Museum of the American Indian: 13/1148   W: 2 ft. 11 in.

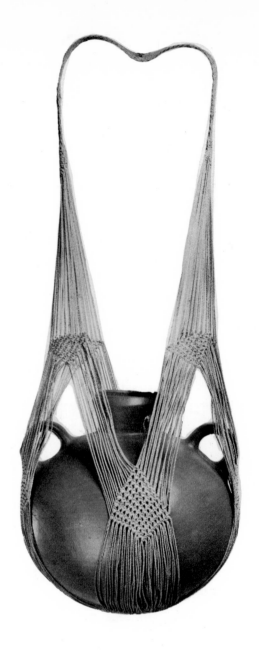

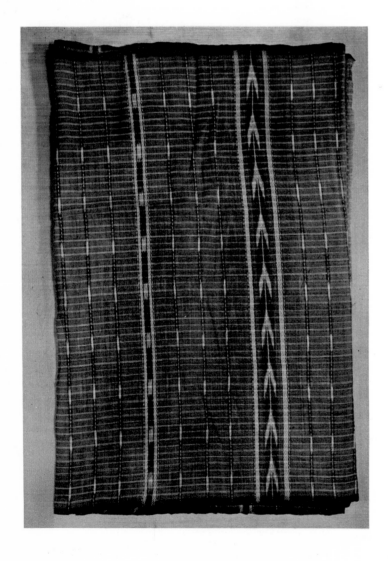

231 *WATER JAR AND NET*

The string carrying net and round redware water jar combine to form a beautifully balanced composition. Separately or together, these show functional beauty. Collected at Guatajiagua in 1924 by Samuel K. Lothrop.

LENCA; Ahuachapán, El Salvador   1920-1924
Museum of the American Indian: 13/1007, 13/1163   Jar: 10 in.

232 *MONKEY EFFIGY JAR*

The modeled features of this redware vessel make an amusing touch to a beautifully formed globular body. This is not unlike certain prehistoric wares from Middle America; if fragments were found separately, it would well confuse the archeologist. See Plate 172. Presented by F. A. Lux.

PIPIL; San Salvador; El Salvador   1930-1940
Museum of the American Indian: 20/5910   H: 11 in.

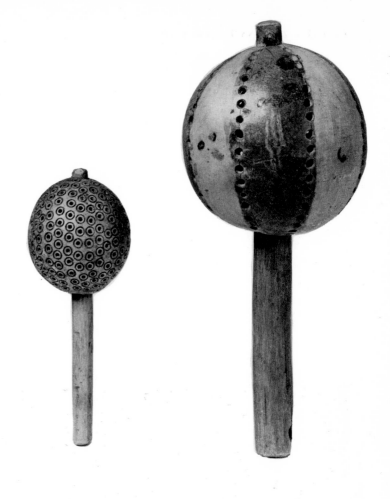

233 *PERFORATED GOURD RATTLES*

These people make a great variety of gourd rattles, decorated with color and perforated designs to form visually attractive, yet efficient, musical instruments. Collected at Yucaiquín in 1924 by Samuel K. Lothrop.

CACAOPERA; Ahuachapán, El Salvador   1920-1924
Museum of the American Indian: 13/1011, 13/1027
            Longest: 8 ½ in.

234 *BARK DANCE MASKS*

A year following the death of a person, spirits representing animals come to take the soul to the hereafter in a major ceremony called *Yapti,* the Feast of the Dead. Remarkable masks, known as *sikro,* are worn on the head at such dances; the fiber skirting conceals the wearer's face. Collected at San Carlos in 1924 by David E. Harrower.

MISKITO; Wanks River, Nicaragua   1900-1924
Museum of the American Indian: 13/2498, 13/2499   H: 35 in.

235 *COTTON SKIRTING MATERIAL*

Although very few Boruca women still weave, their skill is apparent in this example intended for a *manta,* or skirt. Woven of native cotton, the base fabric is decorated by multi-color designs; these are not embroidered, but are single-faced weft-pattern weaving, developed as the textile progresses. Collected at Cabagra by Jorge A. Lines.

BORUCA; Puntarenas, Costa Rica   1930-1935

Museum of the American Indian: 23/2082   25 x 36 in.

236 *WOODEN SKULL MASK*

A wide variety of carved masks are worn by men dancers at the New Year's ceremonies; little is known of the nature of these relatively secret performances. Masks are also worn at the feast celebrating the " birthday " of the death of an individual, held a year following the event. Collected at Boruca by Jorge A. Lines in 1924.

BORUCA; Puntarenas, Costa Rica   1930-1940

Museum of the American Indian: 23/2088   7 x 8 in.

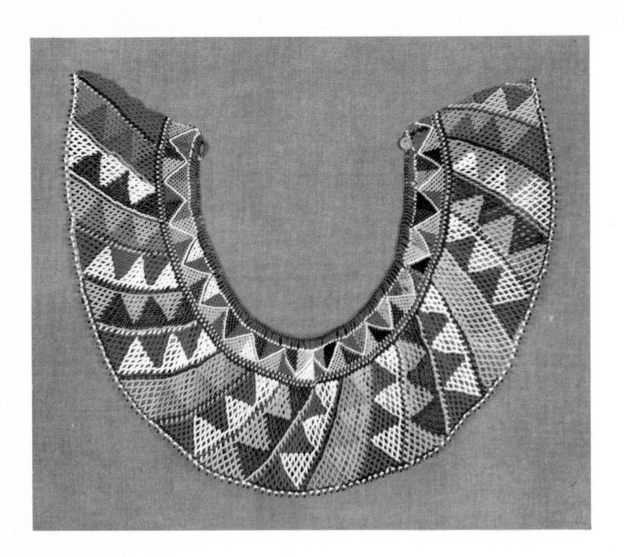

237 MAN'S BEADWORK COLLAR

The netting technique used to make this colorful neck
ornament is of a style found throughout the Americas;
the beads are obtained from white traders. The collars
are traded widely, some even turning up in the southern
United States. These prized possessions of the men are
worn primarily on festive occasions. Presented by Alice
W. Dockstader.

GUAYMÍ; Chiriquí, Panama   1925-1950
Museum of the American Indian: 22/6343   5 ½ x 10 in.

238 BARK-CLOTH COSTUME

Costumes made from sheets of bark cloth are used in
the rapidly disappearing *Kuqua* ceremonies; they include trousers, shirt, and a mask constructed on a base
made from the skulls of the javelina and deer. The
red, yellow, brown, and blue painted designs are more
decorative than symbolic. Collected in 1924 by A. Hyatt
Verrill.

GUAYMÍ; Coclé, Panama   1920-1924
Museum of the American Indian: 13/2988   Mask: 8 x 13 in.

239 INCISED WATER BOWL

Used for various purposes, these vessels are made from the fruit of the calabash tree, and decorated by incising; in the present example, the simple figures are identical to those found on petroglyphs throughout the region. Collected in the Cuvibora Mountain district in 1925 by A. Hyatt Verrill.

GUAYMÍ; Chiriquí, Panama 1900-1925
Museum of the American Indian: 13/7661 D: 6 in.

240 WOVEN CARRYING POUCH

Colorful containers made by the knotless-netting technique are used all through the Middle Americas; one such example is shown here. Often called *valiente* bags, after an early name for this Indian tribe, they are worn slung over the shoulder. Collected in the Cuvibora Mountain district in 1925 by A. Hyatt Verrill.

GUAYMÍ; Chiriquí, Panama 1900-1925
Museum of the American Indian: 13/7643 L: 7 in.

241 *CARVED SHAMAN'S FIGURE*

Men carve these attractive *shurama* figurines for use in curing ceremonies. The designs are largely incidental, although they may have a relationship to the patient as in this effigy of a man and a child. The features are traditional and stylized. Collected along the Chucunaque River in 1929 and presented by Lady Richmond-Brown.

CUNA; Darién, Panama   1925-1930
Museum of the American Indian: 16/6623   L: 14 in.

242 *STORAGE BASKET AND COVER*

The geometric design of this container and its cover is simple, and in keeping with the work of many tribes throughout America. The *kakku* is a prized possession of the women, in which they keep personal objects. Collected at Yape in 1918 by A. Hyatt Verrill.

CHOCÓ; Darién, Panama   1910-1920
Museum of the American Indian: 8/3529   5 ½ x 10 in.

243 *FEATHERED HEADDRESS*

These colorful headdresses are worn only by chiefs dance leaders, or *lele* (medicine men). The technique of manufacture by using a basketry crown and reed plume-holders, as well as the design style, are almost identical to plumed headgear from northern South America, particularly in the Guianas. Collected from the Teguala people along the Samgundi River in 1924 by A. Hyatt Verrill.

CUNA; Darién, Panama   1920-1925
Museum of the American Indian: 12/8700   Crown: 7 in.
     Full L: 30 in.

244 *WOMAN'S APPLIQUÉ BLOUSE*

Familiar to all travelers in the isthmian region, these intricately worked garments are made by an appliqué technique in which tiny bits of cotton cloth are sewn on to a cut-work cloth base. The *mola* is made by fastening two such panels together with a plain yoke, to form a slip-over blouse. Collected along the Chucunaque River in 1929 and presented by Lady Richmond-Brown.

CUNA; Darién, Panama   1920-1925
Museum of the American Indian: 16/6425   20 x 24 in.

245 *SHAMAN'S CURING FIGURE*

Another *shurama* figure, used in treating illness, this is typical of many patterned after a William Paterson, who attempted to establish a colony of Europeans among the Cuna early in the 18th Century. Apparently he so impressed the Indians that they made figurines in his image for years afterwards. Collected among the Teguala of Chucumbali River in 1919 by A. Hyatt Verrill.

CUNA; Darién, Panama   1915-1920
Museum of the American Indian: 12/7610   L: 15 in.

246 CARVED HARDWOOD STAFFS

Such carefully carved batons, called *kava turgana,* are used as insignia of chieftainship, or occasionally as a medicine staff. They are carved from snakewood in many designs, and are usually about 20 inches long over-all. The longest specimen was presented by Francis E. Ross; the rest were collected by Arne Arbin in 1913.

CHOCÓ; Darién, Panama   1910-1920

Museum of the American Indian: Largest figure: 6 in.
    23/2123, 18/4669, 18/4671, 18/4672

247 GIRL'S SPIRIT IMAGE

Flat carved boards, painted in brown or black, are made in a variety of designs and are given to little girls. These are intended to protect her from harm or illness, and to assure long life; she carries the charm in her arms during ceremonies. This balsa wood image was collected in 1933 by Arne Arbin.

CHOCÓ; Darién, Panama   1930-1933
Museum of the American Indian: 18/4673   L: 12 in.

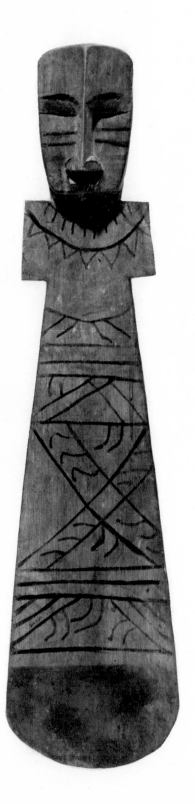

248 BASKETRY CROWN

Pieces of carved and painted balsa wood are inserted into a basketry rim and made into a special type of headdress, worn principally by the women dance leaders. The careful cutting of the black and yellow slats and their fitting into the headband creates a particularly pleasing effect. Collected along the Capetí River by A. Hyatt Verrill.

CHOCÓ; Darién, Panama   1910-1920
Museum of the American Indian: 8/3570   10 x 12 in.

BIBLIOGRAPHY

This listing does not pretend to furnish a complete bibliography of works on Middle American art; it is simply intended to introduce the reader to background resources pertinent to the several regions treated in this volume. A definite effort has been made to include titles for most areas and periods, although some regions have been investigated to such a limited degree that writings about them are very sketchy, indeed. Since most of the books listed include individual bibliographies, each will in turn expand the reader's horizon.

Only book-length works have been listed; with but a few exceptions, specialized archaeological studies and catalogues of museum exhibitions have been excluded for lack of space. Those titles marked* will present the reader with particularly helpful or well-illustrated material, and in total should constitute a basic visual introduction to the Indian art of Middle America.

ANDERSON, LAWRENCE, *The Art of the Silversmith in Mexico, 1519-1936*. New York: Oxford University Press (1941), 2 vols.

ASHTON, DORE, *Poets and the Past*. New York: André Emmerich (1959), 66pp.

*ATL, DR., [GERARDO MURILLO], *Las Artes Populares en México*. México, D.F.: Publicaciones de la Secretaria de Industria y Comercio (1922), 2 vols.

BALSER, CARLOS, *Pre-Columbian Jade in Costa Rica*. San José: Librería Lehmann (1958), 18pp., and 9 plates.

*BASLER, ADOLPHE, and ERNEST BRUMMER, *L'art Précolombien*. Paris: Librairie de France (1928), 63pp., and 190 plates.

BENNETT, WENDELL C., and ROBERT M. ZINGG, *The Tarahumara*. Chicago: University of Chicago Press (1935), 412pp.

BERGSØE, PAUL, *The Metallurgy and Technology of Gold and Platinum among the Pre-Columbian Indians*. Copenhagen: Danmarks naturvidenskabelige samfund (1937), 44pp.

*BERNAL, IGNACIO, *Bibliografía de Arqueología y Etnografía; Mesoamérica y Norte de México, 1514-1960*. México, D.F.: Instituto Nacional de Antropología e Historia, Memorias VII (1962), 1634pp.

BLOM, FRANS, and OLIVER LaFARGE, *Tribes and Temples*. Tulane: Middle American Research Institute (1926), 2 vols.

BOVALLIUS, CARL, *Nicaraguan Antiquities*. Stockholm: P. A. Norstedt söner (1886), 50pp., and 41 plates.

BRAINERD, GEORGE W., *The Archeological Ceramics of Yucatan*. Berkeley: Anthropological Records, No. 19 (1958), 378pp.

*BRENNER, ANITA, *Idols Behind Altars*. New York: Payson and Clarke, (1929), 359pp.

BUNZEL, RUTH, *Chichicastenango; a Gautemalan Village*. New York: American Ethnological Society, Monograph No. 22 (1952), 438pp.

*BURLAND, COTTIE A., *Art and Life in Ancient Mexico*. New York: Oxford University Press (1948), 111pp., and 41 plates.

BUSHNELL, GEOFFREY H. S., and ADRIAN DIGBY, *Ancient American Pottery*. London: Faber and Faber (1955), 51pp., and 84 plates.

CASO, ALFONSO, *The Aztecs, People of the Sun*. Norman: University of Oklahoma Press (1958), 125pp.

*——— *Bibliografía de las Artes Populares Plásticas en México*. México, D.F.: Instituto Nacional Indigenista, Memorias I (1950), pp. 83-132.

*——— and IGNACIO BERNAL, *Urnas de Oaxaca*. México, D.F.: Instituto Nacional de Antropología e Historia, Memorias II (1952), 389pp.

CHARNAY, DÉSIRÉ, *The Ancient Cities of the New World*. New York: Harper and Bros. (1887), 514pp.

COE, MICHAEL D., *Mexico*. New York: Frederick A. Praeger (1962), 245pp.

CONZEMIUS, EDUARD, *Ethnographical Survey of the Miskito and Sumu Indians of Honduras and Nicaragua*. Washington, D.C.: Bureau of American Ethnology, Bulletin 106 (1932), 191pp., and 10 plates.

CORDRY, DONALD B., and DOROTHY CORDRY, *Costumes and Textiles of the Aztec Indians of the Cuetzalán Region, Puebla, Mexico*. Los Angeles: Southwest Museum, Papers No. XIV (1940), 60pp.

———, *Costumes and Weaving of the Zoque Indians of Chiapas, Mexico*. Los Angeles: Southwest Museum, Papers No. XV (1941), 23pp.

*COVARRUBIAS, MIGUEL, *The Eagle, the Jaguar and the Serpent*. New York: Alfred A. Knopf (1954), 314pp., and 48 plates.

*——, *Indian Art of Mexico and Central America*. New York: Alfred A. Knopf (1957), 360pp., and 48 plates.

——, *Mexico South; the Isthmus of Tehuántepec*. New York: Alfred A. Knopf (1946), 429pp.

DAVIS, MARY L. and GRETA PACK, *Mexican Jewelry*. Austin: University of Texas Press (1963), 262pp., and 145 plates.

DEBOOY, THEODOOR, *Archeology of the Virgin Islands*. New York: Museum of the American Indian, Indian Notes and Monographs, Vol. I, No. 1 (1919), 100pp.

*DÍAZ DEL CASTILLO, BERNAL, *The Discovery and Conquest of the New World, 1517-1521*. New York: Grove Press (1958).

*DISSELHOFF, HANS D., and SIGVALD LINNÉ, *The Art of Ancient America*. New York: Crown Publishers (1960), 274pp.

DÖRNER, GERD, *Folk Art of Mexico*. New York: A. S. Barnes (1962), 68pp., and 28 plates.

*DRUCKER, PHILIP, *La Venta, Tabasco: a Study of Olmec Ceramics and Art*. Washington, D.C.: Bureau of American Ethnology, Bulletin 153 (1952), 257pp., and 66 plates.

——, ROBERT F. HEIZER, and ROBERT J. SQUIER, *Excavations at La Venta, Tabasco, 1955*. Washington, D.C.: Bureau of American Ethnology, Bulletin 170 (1959), 312pp., and 63 plates.

*EMMERICH, ANDRÉ, *Art Before Columbus; the Art of Ancient Mexico*. New York: Simon and Schuster (1963), 256pp.

ENCISO, JORGE, *Design Motifs of Ancient Mexico*. New York: Dover Publishers (1953), 153pp.

FERNÁNDEZ, JUSTINO, *Arte Mexicano; de sus Orígines a Nuestros Días*. México, D.F.: Instituto de Investigaciones Estéticas (1958), 208 pp., and 224 plates.

*FEUCHTWANGER, FRANZ, and IRMGARD GROTH-KIMBALL, *The Art of Ancient Mexico*. New York: Thames & Hudson (1954), 125pp., and 109 plates.

*FEWKES, JESSE W., *The Aborigines of Porto Rico and Neighboring Islands*. Washington, D.C.: Bureau of American Ethnology, 25th Annual Report (1907), pp. 3-220, and 113 plates.

*——, *A Prehistoric Island Culture Area of America*. Washington, D.C.: Bureau of American Ethnology, 34th Annual Report (1922), pp. 35-271, and 120 plates.

FOSHAG, WILLIAM, *Mineralogical Studies on Guatemalan Jade*. Washington, D.C.: Smithsonian Institution, Miscellaneous Collections, Vol. 135, No. 5 (1957), 60pp., and 4 plates.

GABB, WILLIAM M., *On the Indian Tribes and Languages of Costa Rica*. Philadelphia: American Philosophical Society, Proceedings, Vol. XIV (1875), pp. 483-602.

GAGINI, CARLOS, *Los Aborígines de Costa Rica*. San José: Trejos Hermanos (1917), 206pp.

GANN, THOMAS W. F., *The Maya Indians of Southern Yucatan and Northern British Honduras*. Washington, D.C.: Bureau of American Ethnology, Bulletin 64 (1918), 146pp., and 28 plates.

——, *Mounds in Northern Honduras*. Washington, D.C.: Bureau of American Ethnology, 19th Annual Report, Part 2 (1902), pp. 655-692, and 10 plates.

*GORDON, GEORGE B., *Examples of Mayan Pottery in the Museum and in Other Collections*. Philadelphia: University Museum (1925-1928), *portfolio, in two parts*.

——, *Prehistoric Ruins of Copán, Honduras*. Cambridge: Peabody Museum, Memoirs I, No. 1 (1896), 48pp., and 8 plates.

——, *Researches in the Uloa Valley*. Cambridge, Mass.: Peabody Museum, Memoirs I, No. 4 (1898), 44pp., and 12 plates.

GROTH-KIMBALL, IRMGARD, *Mayan Terracottas*. New York: Frederick A. Praeger (1960), 45 plates.

Handbook of the Robert Woods Bliss Collection of Pre-Columbian Art. Washington, D.C.: Dumbarton Oaks (1963), 78pp., and 26 plates.

D'HARCOURT, RAOUL, *Primitive Art of the Americas*. Paris: Editions du Chêne (1950), 199pp., and 4 plates.

*HARRINGTON, MARK R., *Cuba Before Columbus*. New York: Museum of the American Indian, Miscellaneous No. 17 (1921), 2 vols.

*HARTMAN, C. V., *Archaeological Researches in Costa Rica*. Stockholm: Ivan Haeggströms boktryckeri (1901), 195pp., and 87 plates.

——, *Archaeological Researches on the Pacific Coast of Costa Rica*. Pittsburgh: Carnegie Museum, Memoirs III, No. 1 (1907), 188pp., and 47 plates.

*HAY, CLARENCE L., *et al.*, [eds]., *The Maya and their Neighbors*. Salt Lake City: University of Utah Press. Revised edition (1962), 606pp.

HEWETT, EDGAR L., *Ancient Life in Mexico and Central America*. New York: Tudor Publishing Co., (1943), 364pp., and 40 plates.

HOLMES, WILLIAM HENRY, *Ancient Art of the Province of Chiriquí, Colombia*. Washington, D.C.: Bureau of American Ethnology, 6th Annual Report (1888), pp. 3-187.

——, *Archaeological Studies among the Ancient Cities of Mexico*. Chicago: Field Museum, Anthropological Series I, No. 1 (1895), 338pp,. and 57 plates.

——, *Handbook of Aboriginal American Antiquities*. Washington, D.C.: Bureau of American Ethnology, Bulletin 60 (1919), 380pp.

——, *The Use of Gold and Other Metals among the Ancient Inhabitants of Chiriquí, Isthmus of Darién*. Washington, D.C.: Bureau of American Ethnology, Bulletin 3 (1887), 27pp.

JOYCE, THOMAS A., *Central American and West Indian Archaeology*. London: P. L. Warner (1916), 270pp.

——, *Maya and Mexican Art*. London: "The Studio" (1927), 191pp., and 61 plates.

——, *Mexican Archaeology*. London: Medici Society (1914), 384pp., and 30 plates.

*KELEMEN, PÀL, *Mediaeval American Art*. New York: Macmillan (1953; 1956), 414pp., and 308 plates.

KELLY, ISABEL T., *Excavations at Apatzingan, Michoacán*. New York: Viking Fund Publications, No. 7 (1947), 228pp.

KIDDER, ALFRED VINCENT, *The Artifacts of Uaxactún, Guatemala*. Washington, D.C.: Carnegie Institution of Washington, Publication No. 576 (1947), 76pp., and 87 plates.

——, JESSE D. JENNINGS, and EDWIN M. SHOOK. *Excavations at Kaminaljuyú, Guatemala*. Washington: Carnegie Institution of Washington, Publication No. 561 (1946), 284pp.

*KIDDER, ALFRED VINCENT, II, and CARLOS SAMAYOA CHINCHILLA, *The Art of the Ancient Maya*. New York: Thomas Y. Crowell, (1959), 124pp.

*KINGSBOROUGH, EDWARD KING, *The Antiquities of Mexico*. London: Lord Kingsborough (1830-1848), 9 volumes, *portfolio*.

KRICKEBERG, WALTER, *Altmexikanische Kulturen*. Berlin: Safari-verlag (1956), 616pp.

KRIEGER, HERBERT W., *Aboriginal Indian Pottery of the Dominican Republic*. Washington, D.C.: United States National Museum, Bulletin 156 (1931), 65pp.

——, *The Aborigines of the Ancient Island of Hispaniola*. Washington, D.C.: Smithsonian Institution, Annual Report for 1929, pp. 473-506.

——, *Material Culture of the People of Southeastern Panama*. Washington, D.C.: United States National Museum, Bulletin 134 (1926), 141pp., and 37 plates.

*KUBLER, GEORGE, *The Art and Architecture of Ancient America*. Baltimore: Penguin Books (1962), 396pp., and 168 plates.

LEHMANN, HENRI, *L'art Précolombien*. Paris: Charles Masson (1960), 76pp.

——, *Pre-Columbian Ceramics*. London: Elek Books (1962), 128pp., and 32 plates.

LEÓN-PORTILLA, MIGUEL, *Aztec Thought and Culture; a Study of the Ancient Nahuatl*. Norman: University of Oklahoma Press (1963), 241pp.

——, *The Broken Spears; the Aztec Account of the Conquest of Mexico*. Boston: Beacon Press (1962), 168pp.

LINES, JORGE A., *Bibliografía Antropológica Aborigen de Costa Rica*. San José: Universidad de Costa Rica (1943), 263pp.

LINNÉ, SIGVALD, *Archaeological Researches at Teotihuacán, Mexico*. Stockholm: V. Petterson (1934), 236pp.

——, *Darién in the Past*. Göteborg: Elanders (1929), 318pp.

LONGYEAR, JOHN M., III, *Archaeological Investigations in El Salvador*. Cambridge, Mass.: Peabody Museum, Memoirs IX, No. 2 (1944), 90pp., and 14 plates.

——, *Copán Ceramics*. Washington, D.C.: Carnegie Institution of Washington, Publication No. 597 (1952), 114pp.

*LOTHROP, SAMUEL KIRKLAND, *Archaeology of Southern Veraguas, Panama*. Cambridge, Mass.: Peabody Museum, Memoirs IX, No. 3 (1950), 116pp.

——, *Archaeology of the Diquís Delta, Costa Rica*. Cambridge, Mass.: Peabody Museum Papers, *in press*.

*——, *Coclé; an Archaeological Study of Central Panama*. Cambridge, Mass.: Peabody Museum, Memoirs VII-VIII (1937, 1942), 327pp., 292pp.

——, *Metals from the Cenote of Sacrifice, Chichén Itzá, Yucatán*. Cambridge, Mass.: Peabody Museum, Memoirs X, No. 2 (1952), 139pp.

*——, *Pottery of Costa Rica and Nicaragua*. New York: Museum of the American Indian, Contributions VIII (1926), 2 vols.

——, *Pottery Types and their Sequence in El Salvador*. New York: Museum of the American Indian, Indian Notes and Monographs, Vol. I, No. 4 (1927), 43pp.

——, *Zacualpa; a Study of Ancient Quiché Artifacts*. Washington: Carnegie Institution of Washington, Publication No. 472 (1936), 103pp.

——, *et. al.*, *Essays in Pre-Columbian Art and Archaeology*. Cambridge, Mass.: Harvard University Press (1961), 507pp.

*——WILLIAM S. FOSHAG, and JOY MAHLER, *Pre-Columbian Art; the Robert Woods Bliss Collection*. New York: Phaidon Press (1957), 286pp., and 163 plates.

*LOVÉN, SVEN, *Origins of the Tainan Culture, West Indies*. Göteborg: Elanders (1935), 696pp., and 19 plates.

LUMHOLTZ, CARL, *Decorative Arts of the Huichol Indians*. New York: American Museum of Natural History, Memoirs III (1900, 1904) *in two parts*; 327pp., and 10 plates.

——, *Unknown Mexico*. New York: Charles Scribner's Sons (1902), 2 vols.

MacCURDY, GEORGE G., *A Study of Chiriquian Antiquities*. New Haven: Connecticut Academy of Arts and Sciences, Memoirs III (1911), 249pp., and 49 plates.

*MARQUINA, IGNACIO, *Arquitectura Prehispánica*. México, D.F.: Instituto Nacional de Antropología e Historia, Memorias I (1951), 470pp., and 291 plates.

MASON, JOHN ALDEN, *Costa Rican Stonework; the Minor C. Keith Collection*. New York: American Museum of Natural History, Anthropological Papers, Vol. 39, Part 3 (1945), pp. 189-318, and 49 plates.

Master Works of Mexican Art; from Pre-Columbian Times to the Present. Los Angeles County Museum of Art (1963), 296pp.

*MAUDSLAY, ALFRED P., *Archaeology; in Biologia Centrali-Americana*. London: R. H. Porter and Dulau (1889-1902), 5 volumes.

MEDELLÍN ZENIL, ALFONSO, *Cerámicas de Totonacapan*. Xalapa: Universidad Veracruzana (1960), 220pp.

*MORLEY, SYLVANUS G., *The Ancient Maya*. Revision by George W. Brainerd. Palo Alto: Stanford University Press (1956), 494pp., and 102 plates.

MORRIS, EARL H., JEAN CHARLOT and ANN A. MORRIS, *The Temple of the Warriors at Chichén Itzá, Yucatán*. Washington, D.C.: Carnegie Institution of Washington, Publication No. 406 (1931), 2 vols.

NOGUERA, EDUARDO, *La Cerámica Arqueológica de Cholula*. México: D.F.: Editorial Guaranía (1954), 315pp.

NORDENSKIÖLD, ERLAND, *An Historical and Ethnological Survey of the Cuna Indians*. Göteborg: Commission for Ethnographic Studies, Vol. 10 (1938), 686pp.

*NORIEGA, RAÚL, et al., [eds]., *Esplendor del México Antiguo*. México, D.F.: Centro de Investigaciones Antropológicos de México (1959), 2 vols.

OAKES, MAUD, *The Two Crosses of Todos Santos; Survivals of Mayan Religious Ritual*. New York: Pantheon (1951), 274pp.

OGLESBY, CATHARINE, *Modern Primitive Arts of Mexico, Guatemala and the Southwest*. New York: Whittlesey House (1939), 226pp., and 12 plates.

*O'NEALE, LILA M., *Textiles of Highland Guatemala*. Washington, D.C.: Carnegie Institution of Washington, Publication No. 567 (1945), 319pp., and 130 plates.

OSBORNE, LILLY DEJONGH, *Guatemalan Textiles*. New Orleans; Middle American Research Institute (1935), 110pp.

PARSONS, ELSIE CLEWS, *Mitla, Town of the Souls*. Chicago: University of Chicago Press (1936), 590pp.

*PEÑAFIEL, ANTONIO, *Monumentos del Arte Mexicano Antiguo*. Berlin: A. Asher & C., (1890) 3 vols., and an atlas of 317 plates.

PETERSON, FREDERICK A., *Ancient Mexico*. New York: G. P. Putnam's Sons (1959), 313pp.

PIJOAN Y SOTERAS, JOSÉ, *Historia del Arte Precolombiano; Mexicano y Maya*. Madrid: Espasa-Calpe (1952), 609pp., and 23 plates.

PIÑA CHAN, ROMÁN, *Mesoamérica*. México, D.F.: Instituto Nacional de Antropología e Historia, Memorias VI (1960), 178pp.

——, *Las Culturas Preclásicas de la Cuenca de México*. México, D.F.: Fondo de Cultura Económica (1955), 115pp.

——, *Tlatilco*. México, D.F.: Instituto Nacional de Antropología e Historia, Serie Investigaciones Nos, 1 and 2 (1958), 2 vols., 56 plates.

PORTER, MURIEL N., *Excavations at Chupícuaro, Guanajuato, Mexico*. Philadelphia: American Philosophical Society, Transactions, n.s., Vol. 46, part 5 (1956), pp. 513-638.

——, *Tlatilco and the Pre-Classic Cultures of the New World*. New York: Viking Fund Publications, No. 19 (1953), 104pp.

*PRESCOTT, WILLIAM HICKLING, *History of the Conquest of Mexico*. New York: Henry Holt (1922), 2 vols. And many other editions.

*PROSKOURIAKOFF, TATIANA, *An Album of Maya Architecture*. Washington, D.C.: Carnegie Institution of Washington, Publication No. 558 (1946), 72pp, and 36 plates.

*——, *A Study of Classic Maya Sculpture*. Washington, D.C.: Carnegie Institution of Washington, Publication No. 593 (1950), 209pp.

RAINEY, FROELICH, *Porto Rican Archaeology*. New York: New York Academy of Sciences, Vol. XVIII, No. 1 (1940), pp., 1-208, and 7 plates.

RIVET, PAUL, *Maya Cities*. New York: G. P. Putnam's Sons (1960), 234pp.

ROBERTSON, DONALD M., *Mexican Manuscript Painting of the Early Colonial Period*. New Haven: Yale University Press (1959), 234pp., and 88 plates.

ROUSE, IRVING, *Prehistory in Haiti; a Study in Method*. New Haven: Yale University Publications in Anthropology, No. 21 (1939), 202pp.

——, *Porto Rican Prehistory; Introduction and Chronological Implications*. New York: New York Academy of Sciences, Vol XVIII, Parts 3-4 (1952), pp. 305-578, and 10 plates.

RUBÍN DE LA BORBOLLA, DANIEL F., *Honduras; Monumentos Históricos y Arqueológicos*. México, D.F.: Instituto Panamericano de Geografía e Historia. Publication No. 146 (1953), 98pp.

——, *México; Monumentos Históricos y Arqueológicos*. México, D.F.: Instituto Panamericano de Geografía e Historia, Publication No. 145 (1953), 487pp.

——, and HUGO CEREZO, *Guatemala; Monumentos Históricos y Arqueológicos*. México, D.F.: Instituto Panamericano de Geografía e Historia, Publication No. 144 (1953), 115pp.

*RUPPERT, KARL, *Chichén Itzá; Architectural Notes and Plans*. Washington, D.C.: Carnegie Institution of Washington, Publication No. 595 (1952), 169pp., and 150 plates.

——, J. ERIC THOMPSON and TATIANA PROSKOURIAKOFF, *Bonampak, Chiapas, Mexico*. Washington, D.C.: Carnegie Institution of Washington, Publication No. 602 (1955), 71pp., and 29 plates.

*SAHAGÚN, FRAY BERNARDINO DE, *General History of the Things of New Spain; The Florentine Codex*. Translated and annotated by Arthur J.O. Anderson and Charles E. Dibble. Santa Fé, N.M.: School of American Research (1950—). In 14 volumes; eleven published to date.

*SAVILLE, MARSHALL H., *The Goldsmith's Art in Ancient Mexico*. New York: Museum of the American Indian, Miscellaneous No. 7 (1920), 264pp.

——, *Monolithic Axes and their Distribution in Ancient America*. New York: Museum of the American Indian, Contributions Vol. II, No. 6 (1916), 13pp.

——, *A Sculptured Vase from Guatemala*. New York: Museum of the American Indian, Leaflet No. 1 (1919), 5pp.

*——, *Turquois Mosaic Art in Ancient Mexico*. New York: Museum of the American Indian, Contributions Vol. VI (1922), 110pp., and 40 plates.

*——, *The Woodcarver's Art in Ancient Mexico*. New York: Museum of the American Indian, Contributions Vol. IX (1925), 120pp., and 51 plates.

SHEPARD, ANNA O., *Plumbate: a Mesoamerican Trade Ware*. Washington, D.C.: Carnegie Institution of Washington, Publication No. 573 (1948), 176pp.

SHOOK, EDWIN M., et al., *Tikal Reports*. Philadelphia: University Museum (1958—). Eleven published to date.

SKINNER, ALANSON B., *Notes on the Bribri of Costa Rica*. New York: Museum of the American Indian, Indian Notes and Monographs, Vol. VI, No. 3 (1920), 107pp.

SMITH, A. LEDYARD, *Excavations at Uaxactún, 1931-1937*. Washington, D.C.: Carnegie Institution of Washington, Publication No. 588 (1950), 120pp.

SMITH, ROBERT E., *Ceramic Sequence at Uaxactún, Guatemala*. New Orleans: Middle American Research Institute (1955), 2 vols.

*SOUSTELLE, JACQUES, and IGNACIO BERNAL, *Mexico in Prehispanic Paintings*. UNESCO World Art Series, No. 10. Greenwich, Conn.: New York Graphic Society (1958), 25pp., and 32 plates.

*SPINDEN, HERBERT J., *A Study of Maya Art*. Cambridge, Mass.: Peabody Museum, Memoirs VI (1913), 285pp., and 30 plates.

——, *Ancient Civilization of Mexico and Central America*. New York: American Museum of Natural History, Handbook No. 3 (1917), 238pp.

SPRATLING, WILLIAM, *More Human than Divine*. México, D.F.: Universidad Nacional Autónoma de México (1960), 64pp.

SQUIER, EPHRIAM G., *Travels in Central America*. New York: D. Appleton & Co. (1853), 2 vols.

STARR, FREDERICK, *In Indian Mexico*. Chicago: Forbes & Co. (1908), 425pp.

*STEPHENS, JOHN LLOYD, and FREDERICK CATHERWOOD, *Incidents of Travel in Central America, Chiapas, and Yucatan*. New Brunswick: Rutgers University Press (1942), 2 vols. Many older editions.

*——, *Incidents of Travel in Yucatan*. Norman: University of Oklahoma Press (1962), 2 vols. Many older editions.

*STEWARD, JULIAN H., *Handbook of South American Indians*. Volume 4: *The Circum-Caribbean Tribes*. Washington, D.C.: Bureau of American Ethnology, Bulletin No. 143 (1948), 609pp., and 98 plates.

STIRLING, MATTHEW W., *Stone Monuments of Southern Mexico*. Washington, D.C.: Bureau of American Ethnology, Bulletin No. 138 (1944), 84pp., and 62 plates.

STONE, DORIS Z., *Archaeology of the Northern Coast of Honduras*. Cambridge, Mass.: Peabody Museum, Memoirs IX, No. 1 (1941), 103pp.

——, *The Archaeology of Central and Southern Honduras*. Cambridge, Mass.: Peabody Museum, Papers XLIX, No. 3 (1957), 135pp., and 46 plates.

——, *The Boruca of Costa Rica*. Cambridge, Mass.: Peabody Museum, Papers XXVI, No. 2 (1949), 50pp.

——, *Introduction to the Archaeology of Costa Rica*, San José: National Museum of Costa Rica (1958), 53pp.

——, *The Talamancan Tribes of Costa Rica*. Cambridge, Mass.: Peabody Museum, Papers XLIII, No. 2 (1962), 108pp.

STOUT, DAVID B., *San Blas Cuna Acculturation; an Introduction*. New York: Viking Fund Publications No. 9 (1947), 124pp., and 16 plates.

STRONG, WILLIAM DUNCAN, *Archaeological Investigations in the Bay Islands, Spanish Honduras*. Washington, D.C.: Smithsonian Institution, Miscellaneous Collections Vol. 92, No. 14 (1935), 176pp.

*——, ALFRED VINCENT KIDDER, II and A. J. DREXEL PAUL, JR., *Preliminary Report on the...Archaeological Expedition to Northwestern Honduras, 1936*. Washington, D.C.: Smithsonian Institution, Miscellaneous Collections Vol. 97, No. 1 (1939), 129pp.

THOMPSON, J. ERIC S., *Ethnology of the Mayas of Southern and Central British Honduras*. Chicago: Field Museum, XVII, No. 2 (1930), p. 27-213, and 23 plates.

*——, *Maya Hieroglyphic Writing; an Introduction*. Norman: University of Oklahoma Press (1960), 347pp.

*——, *The Rise and Fall of Maya Civilization*. Norman: University of Oklahoma Press (1954), 289pp., and 24 plates.

*TOOR, FRANCES, *A Treasury of Mexican Folkways*. New York: Crown Publishers (1947), 570pp.

——, *Mexican Popular Arts*. México. D.F.: Frances Toor Studio (1928), 107pp.

*TOSCANO, SALVADOR, *Arte Precolombino de México y de la América Central*. México, D.F.: Instituto de Investigaciones Estéticas (1944), 556pp.

——, PAUL KIRCHHOFF and DANIEL RUBÍN DE LA BORBOLLA, *Arte Precolombino del Occidente de México*. México, D.F.: Secretaria de Educación Pública (1946), 68pp.

TOZZER, ALFRED M., *Chichén Itzá and its Cenote of Sacrifice*. Cambridge, Mass.: Peabody Museum, Memoirs XI-XII (1957) 316pp. and 710 plates.

VAILLANT, GEORGE C., *Artists and Craftsmen in Ancient Central America*. Museum of Natural History, Guide Leaflet No. 88 (1935), 102pp.

*——, *Aztecs of Mexico; Origin, Rise and Fall of the Aztec Nation*. Revised by Suzannah B. Vaillant. New York: Doubleday & Co., (1962), 312pp., and 68 plates.

——, *Masterpieces of Primitive Sculpture*. New York: American Museum of Natural History, Guide Leaflet No. 99 (1939), 10pp.

VAN DE VELDE, PAUL and HENRIETTE VAN DE VELDE, *The Black Pottery of Coyotepec, Oaxaca, Mexico*. Los Angeles: Southwest Museum, Papers No. 13 (1939), 43pp.

VILLAGRÁ CALETI, AGUSTÍN, *Bonampak, la Ciudad de los Muros Pintados*. México, D.F.: Instituto Nacional de Antropología e Historia (1949), 43pp.

VON HAGEN, VICTOR W., *The Aztec and Maya Papermakers*. New York: J. J. Augustin (1944), 120pp., and 39 plates.

*WESTHEIM, PAUL, *Arte Antiguo de México*. México, D.F.: Fondo de Cultura Económica (1950), 356pp.

——, *The Sculpture of Ancient Mexico*. New York: Doubleday-Anchor Books (1963), 69pp., and 96 plates.

WILLEY, GORDON R., and CHARLES R. McGIMSEY, *The Monagrillo Culture of Panama*. Cambridge, Mass.: Peabody Museum, Papers XLIX, No. 2 (1954), 158pp., and 20 plates.

WISDOM, CHARLES, *The Chorti Indians of Guatemala*. Chicago: University of Chicago Press (1940), 490pp.

*WOLF, ERIC, *Sons of the Shaking Earth*. Chicago: University of Chicago, Phoenix Books (1962), 185pp.

WOODBURY, RICHARD and AUBREY S. TRIK, *The Ruins of Zaculeu, Guatemala*. New York: United Fruit Co. (1953), 2 vols.